DON'T STOP...

CANTER INTO

your

PONY ANNUAL

2023

THIS ANNUAL BELONGS TO

Kaede M

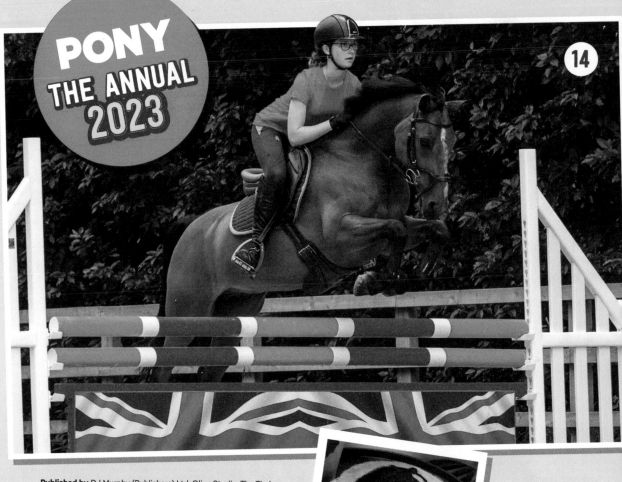

PONY
THE ANNUAL
2023

14

Published by DJ Murphy (Publishers) Ltd, Olive Studio, The Timber Yard, Grange Road, Tilford, Farnham, Surrey GU10 2DQ

Who did what in PONY – The Annual
Contributors Tilly Berendt, Kiera Boyle, Sarah Burgess, Megan Hurley, Louise Kittle, Keeley Mitson
Senior Designer Adam Witt
Designers Jake Booth, Paul Smail
Managing Director Zoe Cannon
Commercial Director Abi Cannon

Who took the pics
Photography Peter Nixon, Jon Stroud, Louise Clarke Photography, Michael Mount Photography, Ultimate Images. (Stock photography courtesy of Birute Vijeikiene, Dcurzon, Englishinbsas, Gertan, Kevin Day, Lois GoBe, Massimo Todaro, Nigel Baker photography, Stefan Holm, Vladmir Wrangel / Shutterstock.com)
Cover photo Lucy Merrell
p102-103 Illustrations by Helen Öhmark and Rebecca Öhmark

PONY magazine is published every four weeks. To find out more about PONY magazine, visit ponymag.com
© Copyright DJ Murphy (Publishers) Ltd 2022

Printed by Graphicom via dell'Industria – 36100 Vicenza, Italy

ISBN 978-1-913787-10-3

RRP £12.99

Make

Marvellous masterpiece on p20!

54

66

Inside... YOUR ANNUAL

Help your dreams come true on p44!

(84)

PROBLEM PONIES SOLVED

Ever wonder why your pony acts the way he does? Well, we've got the answers!

As much as we totally adore ponies, the way they think is super-different to us humans. You may wonder why he finds a flowerpot he's seen a thousand times before so scary all of a sudden, or why he refuses to be caught in the field! Well, the way to find out is by putting yourself in his shoes, and trying to think like he does! We explain all...

THE FRUSTRATING FIDGET

Is there anything more annoying than a pony who just won't stand still when you're trying to groom or plait him? Nope! But why does he like to move about so much? Well, it's usually down one of three things – excitement, nerves or boredom.

Maybe you're at a new place for a competition and he's raring to go, so has ants in his pants? Or it could be that he's feeling anxious about being separated from a friend, or that he's bored of being in the stable and really wants to go out to the field. Whatever the reason, it's important to recognise it, then try to solve the problem.

⊰ FIX IT! ⊱

Why not try...

- **offering him a distraction** A haynet can do the trick to keep your pony happy, but other options include a lick or stable toy. If you can, why not give him a swede or carrot on a string so he can play with it while he stands?
- **giving him a friend** Most horses feel a lot happier if they have a pal to keep them company while they're standing to be groomed
- **identifying how he's feeling** Has your pony been in the stable all night? If so, he's probably full of energy by now! Try to tack him up for a ride or turn him out as soon as possible so he can let some of his energy out, then you can groom him properly later when he's feeling a bit calmer

TOP TIP
Why not get your tack out and ready before you bring your pony in to ride? This will help you feel more organised and reduce the time he has to stand around waiting.

TOP TIP
Try offering him a treat when you approach him in the field. That way, he'll be super-pleased to see you!

THE REBEL RUNAWAY

You walk up to your pony who's grazing in the field – headcollar and leadrope in hand – and he immediately starts trotting in the opposite direction. No matter what, he won't let you get close and now you're late for your lesson!

Does this sound all too familiar? Well, ponies are flight animals by nature, which means they're hardwired to flee from any potential danger. It may be that your pony would much rather stay out and munch tasty grass than come in to be ridden. Perhaps he has a best friend he wants to carry on hanging out with, or maybe he can sense that you're nervous or stressed about something – school, your riding lesson – it could be anything! Don't worry though, there are some things you can do to help.

> *Mix things up so you don't only bring your pony in to ride or for the vet or farrier*

⇒ FIX IT! ⇐

Try some of these to help your pony associate coming in with nice things...

- **make his stable the best place ever** Mix things up so you don't only bring your pony in to ride or for the vet or farrier. Why not give him a long pamper session, or take him for a relaxed walk sometimes? That way, he'll start to look forward to coming in, rather than thinking it means work

- **increase his time out** Most ponies prefer to spend as much time as possible outdoors! So, if you can, allow him to have more time in the field to eat and chill. That way, he'll feel more content in general, and be happier to come in when you want him for something

- **control your breathing** Believe it or not, ponies have the ability to sense your heartbeat! So, if you're breathing's short and sharp, or your heart's beating quickly, he'll think there's danger afoot and look to escape! Try to stay calm and keep your breathing slow and steady whenever you approach him

THE SCAREDY-CAT SCATTERBRAIN

You and your pony are out on a hack but it's a bit windy today. Before you know it, he's leapt to the side because a garden waste bag's blown across the road! If this sounds like your pony, don't worry. Although spooking can feel really unsettling, it's a natural thing that ponies do.

Like we said before, ponies are flight animals who run at any sign of danger. So what looks like a harmless bag to you could easily be a big, green, scary predator jumping out ready to eat him! He might've had a bad experience before that he still remembers, too. But, luckily, there's are some tactics you can try to help him feel more brave.

TOP TIP
For even more awesome tips on how to ride a spooky pony, turn to p24!

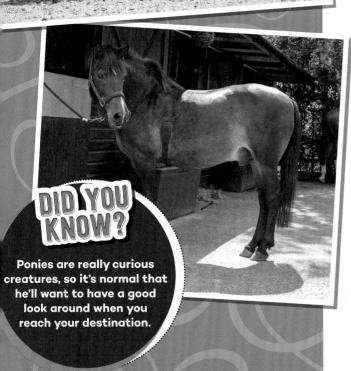

DID YOU KNOW?
Ponies are really curious creatures, so it's normal that he'll want to have a good look around when you reach your destination.

FIX IT!

To help your pony feel more confident and less frightened you can...

- **become a more confident rider** Your pony will look to you to reassure him that everything's okay. So, try to put your brave pants on and use your voice to softly let him know you're there to protect him
- **improve your position** Having a really secure position in the saddle will help you sit to any spooks your pony may throw at you. This will also lead to improving your confidence, which will rub off on him, too!
- **desensitise him in-hand** In the arena, spend time showing your pony different objects and encourage him to check them out. You could teach him to follow you over a wooden plank or tarpaulin, but remember it will take time for him to build trust in you and relax with these new objects – don't rush him

THE NOSY NEWCOMER

Does your pony have his eyes on stalks whenever you take him somewhere new? Well, if you can't get any sense out of him when you first arrive at a lesson or show, it's likely because his brain's taking in so many sights, sounds and smells that he can't focus on you. He may also be feeling a bit nervous and confused because he doesn't know what's about to happen or why he's there.

FIX IT!

To help your pony feel more confident when he's out and about, try..

- **staying really calm** Your pony will feed off you if you're nervous, so staying ultra-chilled will help him learn there's nothing to be worried about
- **taking him out more often** As well as giving your pony time to look around on arrival, over time he'll become more accustomed to going to new places if you do it more often. You could take the pressure off by going to hire an arena or for a super-fun hack so he has a really nice time
- **bring a friend along** Sometimes, having a familiar buddy from home can help him feel more calm because he has someone he knows to support him

LET'S GO RACING

Speed, stamina and even Shetlands... get the low-down on pony racing

Horse racing's one of the biggest spectator sports in the world, but did you know there are also races dedicated to ponies? Pony racing's an adrenaline-filled sport that's just as competitive and exciting as horse racing. It's also accessible to everyone – you don't even need your own pony to take part!

Perfectly paced ponies

Back in 2007, the Pony Racing Authority was formed to support young jockeys. It holds races across the country, at some of the most prestigious venues, for people from all backgrounds. It's always had close links with the Pony Club, which holds taster sessions, training events and race days. So, if you fancy giving pony racing a go, why not speak to someone at your local Pony Club branch to find out more?

Super-speedy Shetlands

There's nothing more exciting to watch than cute, fluffy and surprisingly quick Shetlands racing their hearts out over a course of mini brush fences. The Shetland Pony Grand National (SPGN) is a highly anticipated event and each year at the London International Horse Show (LIHS), 11 jockeys and their ponies take to the stage and race for the title. To compete at LIHS, jockeys must qualify at five other races throughout the year. But the challenge of Shetland racing doesn't stop there – once they've qualified, they have to raise at least £1,000 for the organisation's chosen charity.

Fit the bill

Although you don't need your own pony to take part, you do have to meet the age and height requirements if you want to turn your hand to Shetland pony racing. Jockeys must be 8–14 years old to get involved and they can't be more than 1.52m tall, because the ponies are so small!

But pony racing's slightly different – it's all to do with age and weight. The max age is 16 and weight depends on the height of your pony. If you're super-light, he'll be able to go faster, so this rule stops some jockeys having an unfair advantage!

DID YOU KNOW?

Nell Stephens is the youngest jockey to win a SPGN. At Olympia in 2019, at the age of nine, she took the title, beating the favourite – how amazing!

Sizing up

There are obviously rules and regs for the ponies, too. You've probably already guessed it, but races are only open to ponies who are 14.2hh or under. The Joint Measurement Board is an organisation dedicated to accurately measuring horses and ponies – its job is super-important and determines which ponies can and can't race.

The ponies must be 5–20 years old and as fit as a fiddle. Vets play an important part in the welfare of the ponies – if they're on the older side of life, they might be restricted to just taking part in display races, which are a lot less intense.

WINTER CHECKLIST

Tick off important to-dos to keep your pony healthy in the winter months

TOP TIP
If you have any concerns about your pony's health, contact your vet.

For most people, thoughts of winter include snow, Christmas and cosy fireplaces. But for pony lovers, all we see is mud, rain and dirty coats! As a result of the changing weather, there are several things it's important to check regularly to ensure your pony thrives during the cold season. Let's take a look.

☐ Save his skin

Your pony's skin's exposed to the elements while he's out in the wind, rain and mud, which means it can easily become damaged. It's important to help keep it healthy by checking for any changes to his skin. Winter conditions that can affect him include...

- **mud fever** is a bacterial infection that can happen when your pony's legs when exposed to wet conditions. If he's prone, you can reduce the chance of a flare-up by using barrier creams or pig oil on his lower legs to protect him from the wet and mud. Avoid hosing his legs too often, as this can weaken the skin. Instead, leave the mud to dry and brush it off later

- **rain scald** is caused by the same bacteria as mud fever, but occurs on the back and hindquarters. You might find scabs when grooming, which are a tell-tale sign. Make sure your pony has adequate shelter from the elements and that he's not wearing too heavy a rug, because being warm and damp under a rug makes rain scald much more likely to happen

- **rug rubs** can happen if a rug doesn't fit well or is left on for too long. It's important to regularly give your pony time without a rug, and look out for any signs of rubbing so you can treat them early. Using a soft bib can also help

Hoof it

Winter's a common time for hoof problems, so taking extra care of your pony's feet is vital. It's extra important to carefully pick out his feet every day – if they begin to smell bad, this could be a sign of thrush, so speak to your yard manager straight away. You can use hoof conditioners to keep his hoof wall healthy – speak to your farrier to find out the best one for your pony's hooves.

Field inspection

Bad weather can wreak havoc on your pony's paddock, so making daily checks is extra important for his safety. Look out for...
- broken or loose fence posts, or damage to hedges or electric fences
- dirty or icy water troughs
- ruts or holes
- poached areas

Sorting out potential hazards quickly will help your pony stay safe, so keep an eye out!

Breathe a sigh of relief

Lots of ponies spend a bit more time in their stables over the winter months, meaning they eat more hay than grass. This cause problems for your pony's airways. If you notice he starts coughing, or is breathing differently, it could be a sign that he's struggling with the dust in his environment.

Ensure his stable's kept free from dirty bedding and always remove him from the stable before you muck out or sweep, so he's not breathing in more dust or spores. You can soak or steam his hay, or even switch to haylage – speak to your yard manager to work out what's best.

Get on schedule

Winter's a brilliant time to give your pony a full check over before the summer season comes around. So, check when he's next due for his vaccinations and teeth and book him in with your vet. You can also make an appointment with your physio and saddle fitter so he's ready to go out and have loads of fun come spring.

DID YOU KNOW?

Many vet practices offer a winter health MOT, which includes all the vital checks, such as his eyes, heart and bloods, alongside his annual booster and teeth.

CRYSTAL CLEAR

Set yourself up for success and jump the perfect clear round every time

The buzz of jumping a clear round is like no other, but the simplest of mistakes can be the difference between topping the leaderboard and facing elimination. Check out our tips on how to ace your next comp, so you can keep your eyes on the prize and your pony performing at his best.

1
Schedule regular jumping lessons so you always have something to work on and look forward to. Be sure to practise outside of lessons, but don't jump all the time as it puts strain on your pony's body and can make him sour.

2
Use exercises to improve your pony's technique, athleticism and strength – such as high-sided cross-poles and v-poles. You can also add raised poles, bounces and grids into your schooling sessions to keep him supple and gradually build up his muscles.

3
During your training sessions make sure your pony sees a variety of fences. You won't always know what you'll meet on the course – it could be planks, fillers, water trays or skinnies – so making sure he's seen them all and can jump confidently will give you the upper hand.

4
Don't forget about your flatwork – it's so important! Focus on creating a punchy canter that's forward but not flat, and try lengthening and shortening strides. That way, when it comes to related distances, you'll be able to ride them perfectly every time.

5

It's best to compete at a lower height than what you're practising at home to make sure you feel confident. Check out the schedule in advance so you can plan what classes you'll enter, then tailor your training to set you up for success.

6

Walking the course properly is key! Avoid wandering round just to work out the order of the fences. Remember to take note of distances, turns and any tricky or spooky fences that your pony might hesitate at. Then, plan how you're going to ride each element of the course.

7

The aim of your warm-up is to prepare your pony physically and mentally – work on getting his muscles into gear and his mind on the job. Use the time to make sure he's responding to your aids, but don't use up all his energy before you head into the ring.

8

Stick to your plan! Try to ride every line and corner exactly as you'd planned. If you spontaneously decide to cut corners or change your line, you might make a mistake that could cost you a clear. There's no problem with doing tight turns in a jump-off, just make sure you plan them while walking the course so you can give your pony clear instructions.

9

As you're riding around the course, encourage your pony to land on the correct leg after each fence. Landing on the wrong leg will make him feel unbalanced on the turn, which could affect how he jumps the next fence. You can practise this easily at home over a single fence, just change it up and give him clear signals so he lands correctly.

10

On the approach, remember to keep your shoulders back and look ahead! If you keep your eyes up and sit tall, it'll do wonders in helping your fave pony jump clear. Leaning too far forwards on take-off and looking down at the fence could encourage him to drop his shoulder and lose balance, meaning he'll find it tricky to pick up his legs quickly.

OWN-A-UNICORN DAY

When Faye's invited to the unicorn stables, she discovers that not everything's what it seems

Most children dream of going for their first pony, or maybe even donkey, ride – but not Faye. After weeks of tryouts in all different disciplines, from cloud hopping to rainbow spotting and even unicorn anatomy, Faye was selected for the final exam that would secure her a place at her dream school – the Above the Clouds Centre of Magical Excellence. She had to attend an own-a-unicorn day and to prove her knowledge of unicorn care and flying ability once and for all. And she was super nervous.

Registration

Faye glanced around in awe as she stepped through the golden gates that marked the entrance to the unicorn stables. She was in a group with seven others, but only half would be selected to study at the school. Everyone had their most serious game faces on – it was apparent they wanted to be a pupil here as much as Faye did.

Her eyes sparkled as she took in the best view in the world – unicorn heads of all different pastel colours, snorting and whickering over stable doors. Each one had a unique-looking horn, and all of them glistened in the sunlight.

A stern-looking figure emerged from one of the stables. Her black bun was scraped back to the max, and she had an ominous clipboard hugged into her chest. "My name's Ms Featherton," the lady explained, "and I need each of you to raise your hand when I call your name and go to the stable I allocate you to". Everyone remained deadly silent.

An unexpected pairing

Ms Featherton reeled off unicorn names – Lightning Lily, Diamond Disco, Rainbow Rocket – but Faye's unicorn wasn't called until last. "Faye Buchanan, you have Peg." *Peg?* she thought. *That doesn't sound much like a unicorn.* Nonetheless, she walked over to the stable with the corresponding brass nameplate and glanced over the door. Sure enough, she wasn't

met with a unicorn at all. Instead, there stood a short, steel grey pony. He looked utterly ordinary, and didn't even have a horn! Faye apprehensively walked back over to Ms Featherton and explained that there must have been a mix-up. "No mistake, Miss Buchanan. Now, you'd better get started on the mucking out challenge before you fall behind."

Mucking in

The idea of own-a-unicorn day was just that – you had to prove you could own your own unicorn. So, naturally, the first challenge tested how well you could muck out a stable. Unicorn bedding was a bit like candy floss in texture and unicorn poo was blue and gooey, like cupcake icing – very different from a standard pony. Luckily, Faye was a pro at mucking out unicorn beds, so this would be a piece of cake.

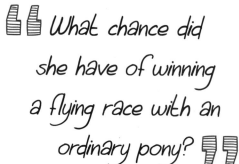

What chance did she have of winning a flying race with an ordinary pony?

However, when she stepped into Peg's stable, she was caught by surprise. It looked just like a normal pony's stable! He was on a bed of straw and had regular brown pony droppings.

Peg blinked at her. Though he was plain in appearance, he had the most enormous eyes that Faye couldn't help but smile at. Even though he clearly wasn't a unicorn, he gave her a warm feeling. She guided him out of the stable and tied him alongside the unicorns in the middle of the yard. He was tiny compared to the others, but Faye kissed his nose and gave him a cuddle anyway, before starting the challenge. Working off what she knew of unicorn beds, Faye mucked out Peg's stable as best she could but, when the final buzzer sounded, she wasn't pleased with her work at all. This seemed totally unfair! Nonetheless, Ms Featherton nodded her approval when she inspected Faye's handiwork. Somehow, she moved onto the next phase – unicorn knowledge.

The group was ushered into a classroom while the unicorns – and Peg – munched haynets in their stables. Luckily, Faye's unicorn know-how was on point – her fave thing was reading all about them – so she passed the written exam with flying colours.

As night drew in, the final test began – the twilight flight. Faye's heart sank. What chance did she have of winning a flying race on an ordinary pony?

The twilight flight

This race would be the biggest determiner for who would be accepted at the Above the Clouds Academy, and who would go home empty-handed. Even though Faye thought she'd done well in the other two phases, if she messed up the race her chances would probably vanish. There had to be a reason why she was the only person without a real unicorn. What could it be?

All eight children and their steeds lined up at the start post. They'd have to take off, then dart between the clouds in order to get home in the fastest time possible. *Maybe Peg has a super-fast gallop or something?* Faye thought.

Feeling like she'd lost before she'd even had a chance to try, Faye squeezed Peg on as she cantered him bareback along the misty path. All the other unicorns and their riders quickly took flight, but Peg's feet remained firmly on the ground. Seeing Peg running with all his might, his little legs moving two to the dozen, Faye felt nothing but love for him as he was trying his very best for her. "It doesn't matter whether or not you're a unicorn little Peg, you're just as special to me," Faye whispered to him.

As she patted his shoulder, something truly magical happened. Peg started to rise up, higher and higher. Behind her legs, a pair of enormous wings sprouted from his sides and they flapped up and down with immense power. "Woooo!" Faye cried as she and Peg surged forward. It all made sense now – he was a pegasus!

Faye had tears in her eyes. She'd never seen a pegasus in the flesh because they were so rare that they were on the verge of extinction. Renowned for being the speediest, most agile fliers, Peg effortlessly glided past the other riders, soaring between the markers on each cloud until they reached the finish line, seconds ahead of the rest. As they made their descent, Faye threw her arms around Peg's neck in a huge embrace.

The chance of a lifetime

Faye smiled from ear to ear as the group assembled outside the stables. She was totally overjoyed when her name was called, announcing that she'd earned a place at the school. It'd always been her dream to become a unicorn

jockey but, after her amazing experience with Peg, she was now thinking about specialising in pegasus conservation instead.

After she stepped up to the podium where Ms Featherton handed her a certificate and acceptance letter, Faye was pulled aside. "I'm extremely impressed by how you handled Peg today, Miss Buchanan," Ms Featherton said, mustering as much warmth in her voice as she could. "The reason we allocated him to you was because you're by far the most capable child here, and we wanted to see just how far your talents stretched. Not many people can bond with a pegasus well enough to transform them... but I had a feeling you could."

Faye couldn't stop smiling. "I love Peg, he's taught me so much already."

Ms Featherton smiled. "Indeed," she said. "I'm expecting great things from you, Faye. Use your time here wisely."

"I will," Faye replied. Ms Featherton shook her hand and went back to the ceremony. Faye looked behind her and met Peg's eye, who was watching from his stable. She couldn't wait for all the adventures they were going to have together, here at the school. She knew in her heart they'd be best friends forever.

ON THE HUNT

Spending all day at the yard with pals? We've got a mission for you to complete! Race to see who can gather each item first with our awesome scavenger hunt.

Instructions:

1 Get all your friends together at the start line and get a stopwatch ready.

2 Follow the map and complete the activities or solve the riddle and pick up the items as you go.

3 Ask someone to start the timer as you all set off in a race to be the quickest!

START

ready set go!

Key:

Solve the riddle and pick up the item

Complete the activity

1

Find the place you give your pony a wash,
Splish, splash, splosh!
I carry water around the yard,
Come on! This clue isn't very hard!

2

Pretend to be a pony and canter one lap around the where place you have your lessons.

4 Do 10 star jumps in the place your fave pony spends time grazing with his friends.

3
Head to the place that stores his forage,
Wouldn't this be easy, if he just ate porridge!
Everyday you fill me up,
But I'm much larger than a cup.

5
Go to where your grooming kit's kept,
Hopefully you keep it very well swept.
Pick up the brush that tames his locks,
Then head on to the next box.

6 Sing the alphabet where your pony goes to sleep at night.

7
I live near the place where you empty your wheelbarrows,
Sometimes you'll find one or two sparrows.
I'm used to help sweep the floor,
And I definitely don't fit in a drawer.

8
Head to the room where you make his feed,
When he hears you there he'll start to plead.
Grab the item used to fill his bowl,
Run to the finish, and score the winning goal.

FINISH

PONY PORTRAIT CAKE

Make

Impress your friends with this delicious work of art!

I f you're after a fancy pony-themed cake for your birthday, or can't decide what to make for a charity bake sale, then look no further! Our pony portrait cake not only looks amazing and tastes yummy, it's super simple to make, too.

You'll need

- ✓ two 20cm sandwich cake tins
- ✓ greaseproof paper
- ✓ pencil
- ✓ scissors
- ✓ 200g caster sugar
- ✓ 300g butter, softened, plus extra for greasing
- ✓ 200g self-raising flour
- ✓ 4 eggs
- ✓ 1 tsp baking powder
- ✓ 2 tbsp milk
- ✓ 140g icing sugar
- ✓ cocoa powder
- ✓ black and brown food colouring
- ✓ piping bag or tube with 2mm plain nozzle

Let's get started...

1 Heat the oven to 180°C or 160°C fan and prepare your cake tins. Grease them lightly with butter and cut two circles out of greaseproof paper to fit the size of your tins. On one of your circles, trace the pony portrait template on p101. Then, place the circles in the tins.

2 In a large bowl, mix together 200g of the butter, the sugar, flour, eggs, baking powder and milk until you have a smooth cake batter.

3 Divide the mixture into two bowls. From one half weigh out two lots of 20g of cake batter into two small bowls and colour one black and one brown – add a sprinkling of cocoa powder to the brown one for an extra chocolatey taste!

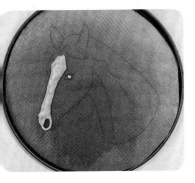

4 To draw your pony portrait, start by adding a small amount of plain cake batter into your piping tube and fill in the pony's blaze and the white of his eye.

5 Next, fill your piping tube with the black-coloured cake batter and draw the pony's nostril, eye, mane and forelock and all the other black lines.

6 Now, get your brown cake batter ready in the piping tube and fill in the rest of the pony portrait.

7 Carefully pour the rest of the plain batter on top of the pony portrait and gently smooth it out so it's level.

8 Add the remaining bowl of mixture to your empty cake tin and smooth the surface.

9 Ask an adult to put the cakes in the oven and then bake for 15-20 minutes, or until golden and the tops spring back when pressed. Once cooked and left to stand for 10 minutes, carefully remove the cakes from their tins. Leave to cool completely on a wire rack.

10 Put the remaining 100g of butter in a bowl and sift in the icing sugar and a tablespoon of cocoa powder, then mix well to make a smooth icing. Spread evenly on the bottom half of the plain sponge. Sandwich the two halves together with the pony on top and there you have it – a pony portrait cake that's sure to wow your pals!

TOP TIP
Have a go at experimenting with different colours and flavours to make a portrait of your pony!

Finished!

THE IRISH SPORT HORSE

Lots of the world's top competition horses are Irish Sport Horses, but these versatile champions can be seen upholding the law on city streets, too!

Rowdy football fans, honking city buses and cycling commuters – none of these things sound like they'd be much fun to encounter out on a hack. But for the horses of the Metropolitan Police's Mounted Branch, it's all part of another day in the office. To excel in the job, a police horse needs to be a few things – super-sensible, sturdy and solid. Enter the Irish Sport Horse.

How to spot them

Irish Sport Horses vary in type depending on how much Thoroughbred blood they have. Top-level event horses have far more Thoroughbred blood, so they're a much finer and sportier model. In contrast, the type preferred for police work are tall and sturdy. They tend to have a lot of bone – strong and large – more like the draught part of their breeding.

DID YOU KNOW?

There are 142 Metropolitan police officers who are trained to ride and, usually, about 110 police horses in the Mounted Branch, which has eight stables across London.

Why the Irish Sport Horse?
A 50/50 combination of a draft breed and Thoroughbred blood gives the horses stamina for a long working day, but also means they're bigger – check out those dinnerplate hooves! It's important that they're big horses, not just so larger policemen can ride them, but they're also used for crowd control, where they command more respect. The breeding's also important for their temperament – they need to be responsive to their rider's aids, but not spooky or reactive, and they can't have any vices such as kicking, napping or biting.

What does it take?

It takes several years to become a police horse. Potential recruits undergo an initial assessment and, if they're suitable, they're assigned to a trainer who gets to know them inside and out, and progressively introduces loads of new challenges. Once they've graduated, they're matched with an officer who'll continue their training on the job – which takes around two years. Once trained, the horses are given a 'PH' (for Police Horse) at the beginning of their name and sent out on duty. On any given day, they might be needed for...

- **general patrol** A three-hour shift on the streets of London. Riders perform normal police duties on these shifts and, often, the horses enjoy a bit of fuss from the public, too!
- **ceremonials** They escort the Queen's Guards, or even the Queen herself!
- **crowd control** Mounted police patrol at events and, if needed, create blockades or direct groups of people

A well-earned rest

The Metropolitan Police horses work six days a week, but their time off is taken in style – they're transported to Bushy Park in southwest London to enjoy a taste of tranquillity in the urban countryside.

HOW TO RIDE A...
SPOOKY PONY

Get the best out of nervous and spooky ponies

It's not always easy to ride a spooky pony – you're probably used to him shying away from fillers, dressage boards or invisible monsters in hedgerows! Luckily, we have a few top tips for how to get the best out of a spooky pony, so you're sure to have loads of fun together.

1.
BACK AT IT

Ponies learn by repetition, so the more practise you can get at riding him in different environments, the better. Don't over-do it, though, as this could stress him out. Why not add one different thing each time you ride? This will help him learn that nothing he meets is out to get him, as well as building your confidence in overcoming scary things together.

TOP TIP
If your pony becomes spooky all of a sudden, ask your vet to check him over to make sure he isn't sore.

2. COOL IT

The most important thing is for you to stay calm! If you get stressed or start kicking or pulling when your pony spooks, it'll make him even more nervous. Instead, take a deep breath, reassure him with your voice and a scratch on the wither, and try again. There's no rush – in fact, the more time you take, the more chilled out he'll feel.

FAVOURITE THINGS

What does your pony love doing the most? For example, if he's always spooking at fillers or poles, speak to your instructor, who can help you work out if he needs to build confidence or if jumping isn't his thing. If it's not, then have a go at other things he does like, such as dressage, mounted games or hacking.

TOP TIP

Pop on a neckstrap so you have something to grab if your pony does a big spook so you don't pull on his mouth by mistake.

4. EASY PEASY

Take time and don't ask too much of your pony. For example, keep fences with fillers small, or stick to shorter hacks on routes he knows well. Gradually upping the challenge will build his confidence and reduce the risk of either of you getting a fright. It might feel boring, but you're building the foundations of your pony's confidence, which will help you in the long run.

5. TWIST 'N' SHOUT

A handy way to distract your pony from spooky objects, such as parked cars or a scary banner in the arena, is to bend him away from it. To do this…
1. Ride a straight line on the approach to the object, leaving a metre or two between it and your pony.
2. Use your inside rein and inside leg to bend him away from the object. Turn your head and shoulders away from it, too.
3. Press your legs against his sides to keep him moving forwards and thinking about what you're asking rather than reacting.
4. Use your inside leg to push him back towards the outside once you're past the scary object, and pat him for being good!

6. PAY ATTENTION

It's common for spooky ponies to lose focus quickly, so finding a few easy exercises to regain his attention is really important. Why not try using transitions, leg-yield, circles and changes of direction to regain his focus? You'll have to rely on trial and error to find the perfect recipe for him, but with a bit of time you'll soon have lots of tools in your kit for those days where he's extra distracted.

7. YOU'VE GOT A FRIEND IN ME

Make the most of having friends with confident ponies to give yours a boost! Whether it's taking a lead into a scary fence or past something spooky out on a hack, a friend's pony is a great help. They'll give you boost a confidence boost – plus, everything's way more fun with friends!

WHATEVER THE WEATHER

Have fun at the yard all year-round!

We pony fans love being at the yard, whatever the weather throws at us! But, what could you get up to on those super-hot or soggy days when you've already ridden and aren't sure what to do next? Check out our all-season guide to having fun!

Super summer

We love summer, but super-hot days can mean you don't feel up to much! Why not try these activities? They're fun with friends and ideal for a scorching afternoon...

- **water fight** Crack out those water pistols, team up and get soaked!
- **scavenger hunt** Round up some mates and get planning – you could even try ours on p18!
- **bath time** It's the perfect time to get your pony gleaming with a proper scrub

Smashing spring

The flowers are growing and, if it's not raining, your yard's sure to look sooo pretty at this time of year! Make the most of it with these fun things to do...

- **photoshoot** Make sure your pony looks his best and take some gorgeous snaps for Insta
- **pamper sesh** Give your pony a well-deserved pamper – a thorough groom, stretch out and a good cuddle will go a long way!
- **spruce up your jumps** Wash them off and repaint the poles, wings and fillers ready for summer jumping sessions

TOP TIP
Ask your yard manager before you tackle any spring cleaning jobs to make sure they're happy for you to do them!

Awesome autumn

It might be getting a bit cooler, but the fun doesn't have to stop! There's still tonnes to do, no matter the weather – have a go at...

- **chase me Charlie** You don't even need a pony! Why not have a yard-wide comp?
- **trick training** Ever wanted to have a go at teaching your pony to smile or bow? Now's the perfect time!
- **sponsored event** Charities always need a little extra support, so why not organise a sponsored event to raise some money

TOP TIP
Could you make your pony some brand-new treats out of things you have at home? Carrots, mash and ice can make a fab equine ice lolly!

TOP TIP
Make sure you wear a helmet, gloves and boots when you're vaulting on to make sure you stay safe.

Wicked winter

It might be cold and the days a bit shorter, but there's still lots of fun to be had at your yard! With or without your own pony, why not have a...

- **tack room clearout** You can tidy up, get rid of any extras and make sure you have everything you need ready for the spring
- **pony quiz** Have a yard quiz to test your pony knowledge! There could be a prize for whoever comes out on top, too
- **try vaulting** It's a great way to jump on your pony wherever you are, so pick the smallest pony on the yard and see if you can vault on!

PHOTO FINISH

Take the perfect pic with your pony pal!

Who doesn't love taking gorgeous shots of their pony? Here at Team PONY it's one of our fave things to do! But how do you take stunning pics every time? Check out our top tips for taking photos that'll fool your friends into thinking you've had a pro shoot!

In the background

Choosing the perfect background can make a huge difference to your photos. Look for places without lots mess or extra objects that'll distract from the focus of your pic – your pony! Pretty locations are fab, too, such as blossoming trees, bright green hedgerows or on the top of a hill with a beautiful view.

TOP TIP

Get a friend on hand with treats to help get your pony's ears forward for your photos.

Get in position

Think about where you want you and your pony to be positioned in the photo – right in the middle, off to the side or from another perspective? A slightly different position can make a pic really stand out, so play around with some different angles to find one you love.

Bath time!

Give your pony a good scrub to get him looking his best before you start taking pics. A super-smart and tidy pony will give your pics an extra pop, and remind you of how gorgeous he is! It's a great excuse to give him a bit of a pamper, too.

TOP TIP
Why not choose an outfit to compliment your pony's coat colour or dress up in your fave matchy gear? It'll make your photos look super-cool!

Lights on
The time of day and location in which you take your photos will affect the lighting. Too bright or too dark can cause problems, so aim for a sunny, but not too bright, day if you can. Avoid taking pics under lights indoors, which can make your photos look washed out, or in places with lots of shadows.

Time it right
You'll need to snap your shot at the perfect time, whether that's when your pony's ears are forward or at the perfect point in the trot to see his legs really striding out. This takes practise, so get out there with your phone and put some time into getting the perfect shot on every go.

TOP TIP
Different coloured ponies look better under different lighting so, if you can, play around with lots of ponies to get a feel for what works best.

SCURRY AWAY

Learn all about the fast and furious sport of scurry driving

DID YOU KNOW?
The sport's full name is Double Harness Scurry Driving.

Have you ever watched scurry driving? Perhaps you've caught glimpses at big venues such as Horse of the Year Show or London International, but how much do you know about this adrenaline-fuelled sport? We've got all the info.

Golden rules

Scurry driving is a super-exhilarating sport where two ponies pull a small carriage around an arena in canter or gallop. The driver's job is to navigate the ponies through a course of 10–14 red cones with balls on top set at 170cm apart, including at least one box and slalom element. This requires immense accuracy because they rack up points for knocking any of the cones or balls. The team with the quickest time and fewest points wins!

Two of a kind

Ponies are split into two categories – under 122cm and over 122cm. Most native breeds are suited to the sport, including children's ponies and ex-gymkhana ponies. The key thing is that they're super-speedy, but also trainable with a level temperament. The most popular are Welsh ponies because they're ultra-nippy and nimble, but Shetlands are popular for beginners because you can get a feel for driving with a bit less speed!

It can look really cool if the pair of ponies match in colour and size, but it's more important that they're evenly matched in pace and easily manoeuvrable.

Kitted out

Scurry drivers don't use regular tack like other disciplines. Instead, it requires specialist equipment, including...

- **a scurry vehicle** This needs to have four wheels and a front axel no wider than 130cm so it can fit between the cones
- **a harness** Ponies wear a double harness made of leather or webbing
- **smart clothing** Drivers need to wear appropriate dress, such as a livery jacket and an up-to-standard helmet

DID YOU KNOW?

There are 25 major scurry driving shows across the UK with two championships to qualify for – the National Championships and the Grand League Points Championships.

DID YOU KNOW?

The ponies often have paired names, such as Tom and Jerry, Ant and Dec or Dun and Dusted!

DID YOU KNOW?

Drivers always have a groom on the back to help balance the cart while they make really sharp turns. They need to be super-brave to do this!

Give it a go

Does scurry driving sound like something you'd love to try? Well, even though it's not the most common equestrian discipline, it is a recognised sport in the UK. The Scurry Driving Association (SDA) is the best place to start because it'll be able to point you in the direction of courses you can take to learn! If you want to get competitive, you'll need a cart and a pair of established scurry ponies to get you started.

THROUGH THE EYE
OF A PONY

How does he see?

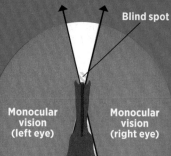

Ever wondered how your pony sees a XC course? Decode his thoughts with our guide

Cross-country's a totally exhilarating discipline, but have you ever wondered what it's like for your pony? Whether he lives for the thrills or he's a little more nervous, we've demystified how he sees different XC obstacles so you can learn how to jump them safely and happily.

What a rider sees

What a pony sees

DID YOU KNOW?

Ponies' eyes are on the sides of their head, meaning they have nearly 360° vision. But they can't see directly in front or behind them.

DITCH THE NERVES

 A narrow, shallow ditch obstacle

 A deep, dark pit of doom that could send me hurtling into the abyss!

One of the biggest pony frighteners on the XC course is undoubtedly the ditch. Riders have a habit of looking down into the dark hole in the ground just as their pony's about to take off – but all this does is encourage him to stop and do the same!

Instead, take a deep breath and try your best to ride it just like you would any other fence. To do it..

1. Pick up an active, steady trot, and keep your approach short so your pony doesn't get too fast.
2. Wrap your legs around his sides and look ahead. Sit up so you're in a secure position, and keep your wrists relaxed so your hands can follow your pony's movement.
3. Squeeze with your legs and allow with your hands – but don't fold into a jumping position – as your pony pops over it.
4. Keep practising until he jumps the ditch without hesitation.

TOP TIP
It can help to imagine there's a rail over the ditch, so you approach it just as you would any other fence.

DID YOU KNOW?

Ponies are said to be colour blind to red and green, which means they don't see those tones like we do. They likely see them as blue or grey!

LEAD A HORSE TO WATER

 A calm, serene puddle that looks fun to splash through

 A whirlpool in a stormy ocean that could be full of sharks, crocodiles or sea monsters!

Splish-sploshing through a water jump is some ponies' fave thing ever, but a nightmare for others! If your pony's a little aquaphobic, it could be because he doesn't know how deep the water will be, or what could be lurking under its surface. The main thing you need to do is reassure him it's okay and keep calm. If he refuses to go in out on course, the best thing to do is take things back a step and work on conquering his fears at home. There are several ways you can do this...

1. Start by working with your pony in-hand – if you can build trust with him, he'll follow you anywhere! Practice encouraging him to walk over strange things, such as a folded tarpaulin or plank of wood.
2. When he's happy doing this, try the same thing while you're riding. Make a point of encouraging him to walk through puddles out hacking or splash through a stream with some other ponies to give him confidence.
3. When you're back on the XC course, go with a friend and pony who will make a good lead and follow them into the water. Start off in walk, and make a big fuss of him when he goes through!

THIN AS A RAIL

 A slightly skinnier fence than normal between two flags

 Nothing! It's so super-thin, how am I supposed to see that?

A skinny jump sits right in your pony's blindspot, which is why it's super-important to ride a straight line towards it. Because he almost has panoramic vision, he'll be able to see much more of the course around him than you, which is why he could be tempted to run out! Luckily, there are some things you can do to help keep him straight...

BABY STEPS

 Some fun little bounces on different levels

 Either a treacherous climb up Mount Everest or base jumping off the Empire State building!

Going up and down steps can be a tricky question for some ponies because they struggle to judge where their feet are going to land next. So, you need to be really positive when asking him to negotiate this type of obstacle to help him balance and understand what he needs to do.

1. Pick up a forward, but controlled canter, aiming for the centre of the skinny.
2. Squeeze your legs around your pony' sides and, while keeping your elbows tucked in, widen your hands to help channel him straight.
3. Look up and ahead of you and don't be tempted to look down on take-off.

TOP TIP
If your pony struggles with skinnies, resting a pole on one or either side of the fence can help discourage him from running out.

Step up

Most ponies find it less scary to go up steps rather than down, so this is a good place to start...

1. Pick up an energetic, punchy canter to power up his hindlegs so he has plenty of momentum to jump up.
2. Keep your eyes up, and make a small fold each time he pops up a step. Stay soft with your hands so he can stretch his head and neck forward to help him balance.
3. Keep your legs squeezed on, especially if there are multiple steps, so he doesn't lose momentum halfway through.

Step down

Your pony might be unsure about stepping down because he won't be able to work out what to do until he's right at the edge of the step, so you need to be extra confident...

1. In walk, squeeze with your legs to encourage him. Don't look down, but be prepared for a sudden jump!
2. As he steps down, lean back and push your lower leg forward. Allow the reins to slip through your fingers a little, too, so he can use his neck for extra balance.
3. On the getaway, sit up and collect your reins again.

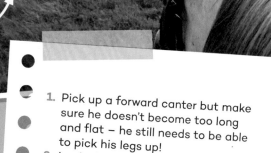

BRUSH IT OFF

 A super-high fence compared to the others

 Easy-peasy! I can just brush my legs through this one

Even though a brush fence may look a little daunting to us, ponies tend to love them! They can tell they aren't as solid as the other fences because they're made of a hedge or branches, so it doesn't matter to them if it looks a little bit bigger. Some brushes even have the middle section cut out, so the raised sides will help encourage your pony to remain central. Here's how to ride them...

1. Pick up a forward canter but make sure he doesn't become too long and flat – he still needs to be able to pick his legs up!
2. Look above the fence and keep your legs squeezed on for encouragement.
3. Make a nice fold over the fence and keep your rein contact soft. Your pony might take a big leap if he's never seen a brush before, but he'll quickly realise he doesn't have to jump the full height.

POLAR PONIES

Bonnie and her family of explorers accidently uncover a brand new species

Bonnie Cartwright's life was pretty cool. She didn't go to school like most children, nor did she stay in one place for more than a few months at a time. Instead, she spent her days travelling the world with her parents. Dr and Dr Cartwright met while they were studying zoology at the University of Cambridge and worked together ever since. Bonnie was born in South America, and shortly after could be found growing up among baby orangutans in the Borneo rainforest. They later travelled to the likes of Botswana, Mauritius, Madagascar, Cambodia, Bali and even Siberia. At the grand age of 11, Bonnie had experienced a lot of the world.

Even though she'd never really had a place to call home, there was one thing that connected every country she visited – ponies. Bonnie's mum was a keen horsewoman, so she got the chance to learn to ride almost before she could walk, and had ridden ponies in nearly every place she went. She mainly rode Western style, and had cantered across the savannah, trekked through rainforests and had been in a horse-drawn sleigh – it wasn't all work, work, work in the Cartwright family.

> **They had the fluffiest coats Bonnie had ever seen**

Globe trotters

The family's next mission would be one of the most exciting yet, and was one that could really put their name into the history books. There'd been a few reports circulating the scientific community about sightings of a possible new breed of penguin in the depths of Antarctica, and Bonnie's parents had been posted to go and investigate.

Bonnie and her mum and dad arrived in their coldest destination to date. It had always been a dream of Liz Cartwright's to visit Antarctica and now she was doing it, with her husband and daughter by her side. But first they had to undergo rigorous training in order to learn how to survive in such a gruelling environment. It was so cold that Bonnie knew that even losing a glove could mean frostbite, or even hypothermia. They were heading to an area of the continent that had only been explored by a handful of scientists. The family of three set up camp on the snowy tundra, exactly as they'd been trained to do. Temperatures were below -20°C, and a storm was moving in. Clad in her specially-designed snowsuit, gloves and balaclava, Bonnie helped her mum build the tent, while her dad got dinner ready. Just as they were finishing and ready to go to bed, Bonnie squinted into the distance. In the rush of snow flakes she swore she could just make out something that resembled a white, swishy tail trotting away from them. Was the cold playing tricks on her mind? Surely it couldn't be... could it?

Adventure awaits

The following day, the family trekked on along the shoreline in pursuit of the new-to-science penguin. The scenery was breathtaking, with icy mountains on one side and the frozen ocean the other. All the while, Bonnie struggled to get what she'd seen last night out of her head. "Mum?" Bonnie asked, as they walked. "Do you think ponies could ever survive in Antarctica?" Her mum chuckled, "I don't see how a pony could live without forage, and there certainly isn't any grass to be seen around here!" Bonnie nodded. Of course a pony couldn't survive out here. What was she thinking? It must have been the snowflakes whirling around. Although she couldn't help but feel a little disappointed.

Finally, they arrived at the spot where they were to set up their base. An expedition team had passed this way a year before and seen signs of penguin life – a broken shell and some droppings unlike any others ever discovered. The Cartwrights got to work, setting up infra-red cameras and taking environmental readings. They had state-of-the-art equipment with some of the most up-to-date technology in the field. If anyone was going to find the mystery penguin, it was them.

Although Bonnie was quite used to these types of expeditions, she always got a little fidgety when it came to the waiting around and gathering data part. But her parents allowed her to explore. There was a tracker in her snowsuit, so they could always locate her if necessary. Being careful not to stray too far from camp, Bonnie decided to explore a snow cave they'd passed a short distance away.

As she got closer she noticed that some of the rocks around the cave mouth didn't have any snow on them. Bonnie's heart lurched at the obvious sign of climate change. It seemed odd, though, because everywhere else around was covered in a thick layer of ice and snow. When she reached the cave, she peered inside, allowing her eyes to adjust to the darkness. Just then, she heard a short, sharp stamp echo through the cave. It made her jump, and it was all she could do not to scream. Reminding herself that the most fierce Antarctic resident was the penguin, she decided to bravely – or perhaps stupidly – venture further inside. As her vision became clearer she was able to make out a huddle of huge penguins standing towards the back of the cave. Edging closer, she stood stock still when she saw them. To her amazement, they weren't penguins at all. They were unmistakably ponies! She took in their bright white fur and mass of mane and tail – they had the fluffiest coats Bonnie had ever seen, which made them look a bit like polar bears. There were three, and lying on the floor asleep – a foal! Trying to contain her excitement so as not to scare the ponies, Bonnie backed away slowly. She had to tell her parents!

A new discovery
Whipping out her walkie-talkie, Bonnie tried to reach her mum. "Mum! Do read me? Over," but the line was crackly and there was no reply. Clambering back across the rocks as fast as her legs could carry her, she was soon back at base. As she described the unbelievable sighting, she was disappointed that her parents seemed so sceptical. "It's like I said, sweetie, how could any equid survive in this type of environment? Are you sure you didn't see some type of seal?"

Bonnie shook her head. "I know what I saw! They're up in the cave, come and see for yourself." But it was getting late, and Bonnie's Dad insisted they have dinner and get some rest. That night, Bonnie tossed and turned – what id the ponies had gone by morning? She knew what she'd seen.

The next morning the family set off to the cave, Bonnie leading the way. "Come on! Quickly!". Her heart was in her mouth as they stopped just inside the opening to allow their eyes to adjust to the dim light – but there they were, resting in almost the same spot. Bonnie's parents were lost for words

History in the making
When the Cartwrights reported their findings to the research organisation, their mission was instantly diverted from possible penguins to tracking the movements of these ponies and finding out as much about them as they could, including how they'd gone undetected for so long.

Bonnie's parents set up night vision cameras and watched the ponies' feeding habits. They seemed to survive on moss that grew in the cave, and sometimes walked to the sea shore to scavenge seaweed washed up by storms. There were so many unanswered questions and Bonnie only wanted to find out more. One day, when they were sitting in the snow watching the ponies forage, the foal strayed closer to them and caught sight of Bonnie. The two of them locked eyes just for a moment before it went bouncing back to its mum. Bonnie couldn't believe she had discovered a new breed of pony that would be written into books and researched forever more. The organisation had even let Bonnie choose a name for the new species. After some consideration, she decided they would be known as Polar Ponies.

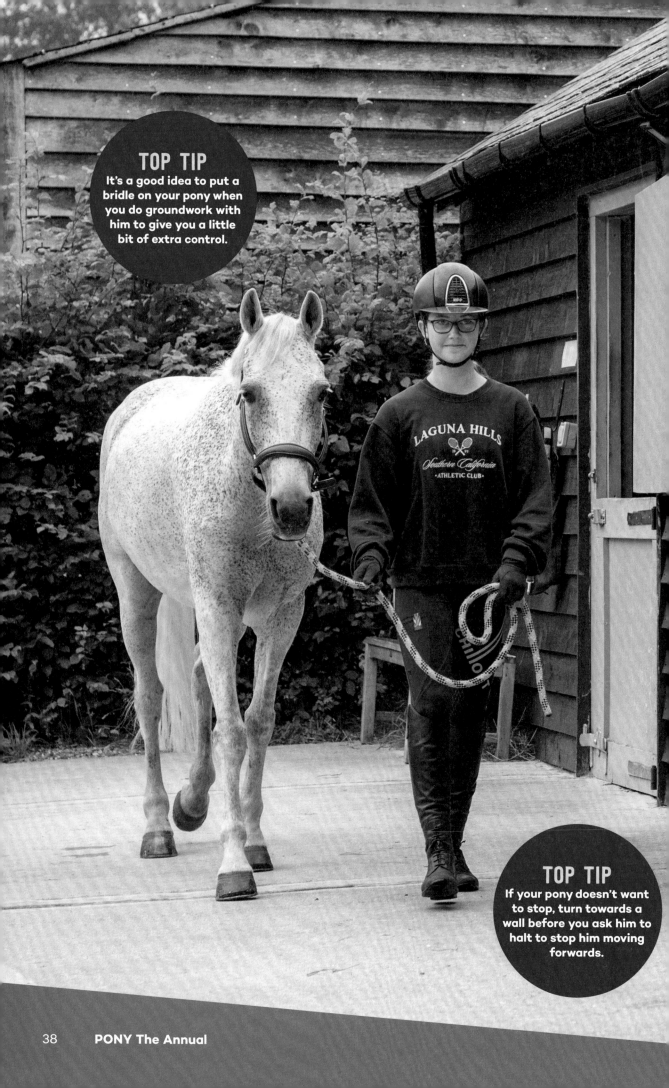

TOP TIP
It's a good idea to put a bridle on your pony when you do groundwork with him to give you a little bit of extra control.

TOP TIP
If your pony doesn't want to stop, turn towards a wall before you ask him to halt to stop him moving forwards.

MIND YOUR MANNERS

Perfect your pony's manners in no time

A pony who's easy to handle will make your life sooo much easier – and it could even boost your ridden work, too. So how can you make sure your pony's manners are top tier? There are no quick fixes, but with a bit of time and patience you'll soon have the best-behaved pony on the yard!

Lead the way

How many times do you lead your pony every week? Whether you're turning him out in the field or taking him to the arena for a quick jumping sesh, you probably lead him more often than you think! Here's how to make it a breeze...

1. Start by walking in a straight line down the yard. Stay next to your pony's shoulder and hold the reins roughly a hand's width below where they attach to the bit.
2. When you're ready, ask your pony to stop by pulling gently on the reins, slowing your steps and saying 'whoa' at the same time.
3. If he doesn't halt immediately, press your spare hand against his chest to make it clear to him what you're asking.
4. Next, say 'walk on' and take a step forward to ask your pony to move again. Try clicking your tongue if he doesn't listen and, if he's really reluctant, carry a schooling whip and give him a gentle flick on his flank when asking him to step forwards.
5. Keep practising moving forwards and stopping until he's listening carefully to what you're asking. Remember to praise him as soon as he responds to your aids so he knows he's done the right thing. ➜

Pick me up

Your pony should be happy to pick his feet up not only for you, but also for your farrier and vet. This will keep everyone safe and make it much easier to keep his feet healthy. So, to make lifting his hooves as easy as pie...

1 Make sure you have your pony's attention. Then, run your hand down the back of his foreleg, or the front of his hindleg.

2 Hold his fetlock and lean against him gently to ask him to pick up his foot. You can add a simple voice command here, too, such as 'up'.

3 He should lift his hoof as soon as you ask. If he doesn't, lean a bit harder or squeeze his fetlock slightly more.

4 When he picks his foot up, praise him, hold his hoof for a couple of seconds and then carefully put it back down. If he tries to pull his hoof out of your hand, hold it up until he relaxes, then put it down.

If your pony's really unwilling to picking up his feet, ask your instructor or yard manager to have a go and see if he's just not listening to you. If they struggle, ask your vet to check him over to make sure he isn't uncomfortable.

TOP TIP
Whether you're working on the ground or under saddle, practice makes perfect! A little bit every day will go a long way.

TOP TIP
If your pony pulls back when he's tied up, don't pull on the rope to bring him forwards. He's stronger than you, and getting into a pulling match will only make things worse. Instead, stand beside him and ask him to step forward.

Barge through

A pony who won't stand still is annoying at best but dangerous at worst. Teaching your pony to listen to you when you handle him will help you have fun together without risking being trodden on! Here are some tips on how to teach him to stand quietly when you ask...

☑ practise moving your pony around on the yard, asking him to stand for a few seconds before moving on again

☑ make sure he moves forward just as quickly as he stops when you ask

☑ once your pony is standing still, keep his attention so he doesn't get distracted and fidget. When he stands, praise him, but be quick to correct him if he wriggles around!

☑ if he moves into your personal space, quickly push him back a step to his original position and reward him when he responds to your command

☑ if you're worried, always lead him in a bridle to keep you safe – you can even use one to lead him to the field

> Grooming sessions or feeding on the yard will help him feel better about being caught

Catch of the day

Is there anything worse than not being able to catch your pony when you're in a rush? We've all been left standing in the field with our pony running rings around us! Luckily, there's lots you can do to make being caught a more pleasant experience for your pony...

- [x] don't only bring your pony in to be ridden. Grooming sessions or feeding on the yard will help him feel better about being caught
- [x] try not to rely on treats to catch your pony, because he's likely to refuse to be caught without them!
- [x] time catching him with when others in his field are coming in, too – then he's more likely to want to come in as well!
- [x] have his tack, teeth and back checked, and arrange for your vet to give him a once-over to make sure he's not sore, because this could make him reluctant to come in
- [x] is your pony getting enough turnout time? If not, he might not want to be caught and have to go back inside so soon

HOW TO RIDE A...
STRONG PONY

Give your arms a break with our tips for riding strong ponies

Some ponies are stronger or heavier in the contact than others – and they can be really tough to ride! It's really important to find ways to keep your pony off his forehand and stop him leaning on you. So, we've put together some tips to help you out.

1.

WHY IS HE STRONG?

The first step is figuring out why your pony's strong. Is he stressed about something? Excited? Uncomfortable? Resisting what you're asking him to do? Once you know why he's acting this way, you and your instructor will be able to find the best solution.

TOP TIP
If your pony suddenly becomes stronger, check all his tack fits him and ask your vet to check him over to make sure he isn't sore anywhere.

2. A BIT OF EVERYTHING

Changing bits won't solve all your problems, but lots of ponies have different bits for hacking, flatwork and jumping, so speak to your instructor and a bitting expert about whether a change could suit your pony. Different mouthpieces with the same cheeks are a good place to start and can discourage your pony from leaning on the bit, making him feel less strong.

3. TURN AROUND

Circles are another good schooling exercise to slow your pony and bring him back to you without having to pull on the reins. Simply sit tall and turn him by looking around the circle and using your inside rein and outside leg to push him around. Using one rein (rather than both) often stops a pony pulling against you, and it can help distract him rather than starting a pulling match!

TOP TIP
Why not stick to canter work uphill? This will make him work extra-hard and help his balance, too!

4. HIT THE GYM

Often when ponies become strong, it's because their muscles are weak and they're relying on you to support them. So, ask your instructor for some schooling tips to help build his strength and help him carry himself. Lateral work, grids and raised poles are really handy places to start!

5. CORE OF THE MATTER

Your pony might be strong, but are you? If you rely on your reins rather than your body and legs, your pony's more likely to pull against you. Instead, work on building up your tummy muscles so you can engage your core and use that to help you slow him down. You don't even have to do a sit-up – riding without stirrups is really effective, too!

6. STOP 'N' START

A good way to make your pony a bit lighter in your hand is with transitions up and down – but especially up. They encourage your pony to sit on his hocks and become less heavy in the contact. You could even add a little bend through the transition to make him work extra hard.

7. FOLLOW THE LEADER

Often, strong ponies prefer to be at the front and can become more excitable if left behind. Explain this to your friends and anyone else you ride with – including the instructor at rallies or clinics. Being near the front could help your pony stay settled and mean he's less likely to rush off and start a pulling match.

UNICORN DREAMCATCHER

Keep your dreams safe with our super-cute make!

Our totally adorable unicorn dreamcatcher is the perfect way to pony-fy your bedroom! It'll look fab hung up above your bed, plus it'll catch all the wonderful pony adventures you go on in your dreams, too!

Make

You'll need
- ✓ cardboard
- ✓ ruler
- ✓ pencil
- ✓ scissors
- ✓ wool
- ✓ white and pink felt
- ✓ glue
- ✓ glitter
- ✓ ribbon
- ✓ felt flowers
- ✓ coloured card

Let's get started...

1 Grab your cardboard and draw a 20cm circle. Draw another larger circle around the first one to make a 1cm wide frame. Then, cut it out to create a ring.

2 Tie your wool in a double knot and wind it all the way around the ring until it's completely covered. Then tie another double knot to secure it.

3 Grab another bundle of wool and start by tying a double knot around a random point on the ring. Then create a web by looping the wool around different points of the ring. Once you've finished the web, cut the wool and tie another double knot to secure it.

4 Cut lots of strips of wool and ribbon – each one around 50cm long – then loop each strip of ribbon through itself along one side of the ring. Bunch up the wool strips into several sections and, like you did with the ribbon, loop them through to allow them to hang down.

5 Draw two triangles onto the white felt to make unicorn ears, and two smaller ones onto the pink felt. Then, cut all four pieces out.

6 Glue the white triangles onto the card (to help make the ears more stable) then stick the pink triangles onto the white ones and cut out the ears.

7 Draw a large triangle, around 15cm long, for the unicorn horn, cover it in glue and stick on the glitter. Let the glue dry, then cut it out.

8 Glue the ears and horn onto the back of the top half of the ring – the opposite side to the ribbon and wool strips.

9 Once the glue has dried, stick the felt flowers on underneath the ears for a lovely finishing touch!

TOP TIP
You can use any materials or decorations you want on your dreamcatcher! Why not add some feathers or beads to jazz it up?

Finished!

45

GET SET FOR SUCCESS

Do your homework and you're sure to get it right on the day!

Whether you're a regular in the comp arena, love going to clinics and lessons, make the most of hacking or are sharing your very first pony, being prepared for every session is a valuable skill. Getting ahead of the game will help you make the most out of every ride – here's how.

Plan it out
Make sure you have a plan for the day – it could be everything you need to bring or timings for getting your pony ready and leaving the yard. This will help you feel super-confident, and leave you stress-free and ready to make the most out of your lesson or comp.

TOP TIP
There are lots of diaries available so you can record your lessons and comps, and see how you've progressed – but a piece of paper and a pen is all you need!

Fit as a fiddle

Are you and your pony fit enough for what you want to do? If you're unsure, scale back your plans, or ask your instructor to take your fitness and energy levels into account by giving you breaks or easier exercises. To boost your pony's fitness...

- do more hacking
- introduce hillwork
- try gridwork and raised poles
- have a go at interval training
- gradually make your sessions longer

Do your homework

Your instructor will give you plenty of things to work on after a lesson – so make sure you practise! This will help you improve and make the progress you want. Knowing you can do it at home first will boost your confidence in lessons and at comps, too, because you'll feel ready for all the new challenges you and your pony encounter.

TOP TIP
Just being in the saddle boosts your fitness. However, pilates, yoga and swimming are all super-fun ways to do it!

TOP TIP
Ask your instructor to write down three things for you to practise after each lesson. That way, you're sure to remember and you can make progress in each session.

TOP TIP
Try to get lots of videos when you can. They'll help you see how far you've come, which is sure to give you a boost!

Positive attitude

It's not always easy, but approaching each challenge with a positive outlook will give you the best chance of success. Instead of thinking about what could go wrong, reframe your thoughts by focusing on what you're looking forward to and how it'll feel when things go to plan! Imagine jumping an amazing clear or mastering those tricky canter transitions and you're halfway to getting it right on the day!

Practice makes perfect

Know what you'll have to do on the day – whether that's what'll be in your dressage test, how big you'll need to jump, or the sorts of things you might meet on your next hack. When you know what's coming up, you can have a go at home.

Enjoy it!

The most important thing is to enjoy what you're doing! The big day is such a small part of everything you do with your pony, so make sure you enjoy the prep that gets you there, too. Nobody loves every second of pony ownership – there are always good and bad days. But, it should mostly be fun so, if you're not having an amazing time, think about ways to make it better – do more with friends, step down a level to boost your confidence or have more lessons to help you improve.

Watch out!

Check out videos and advice from other riders to help give you a boost. They'll have loads of ideas to improve your riding and your pony's way of going, plus top tips for all your equine activities. They'll have seen it all before, so you'll get loads of great advice for things you don't know. For example, you could watch another rider run through your dressage test or jump at the venue you're visiting that weekend.

DID YOU KNOW?

Films and TV shows have strict requirements about what they need their horses to look like – and so stunt horses often get dyed completely different colours for jobs!

THE ANDALUSIAN

They might not have their own category at the Oscars (yet), but filmstar horses always know how to steal a scene. Meet the Spanish breed that excels in front of the camera...

Period dramas might not be your fave watch, but seeing the clever four-legged actors gallop across a field with a lady riding side-saddle or charge into battle is fascinating. Rightly so, too – stunt horses undergo years of training to be able to perform mind-blowing tricks and make movie magic happen. All sorts of breeds are used for stunt work, but the most common is the PRE, short for Pura Raza Española and commonly known as the Andalusian.

How to spot them

Andalusians are one of the most distinctive breeds in the world. With their thick, arched necks, flowing manes and noble, slightly Roman noses, they look totally and completely the part, whether they're playing war horses, fantasy mounts, or the fancy hacks of lords and ladies. At around 15–16.2hh, they're also the perfect size for most actors.

Why the Andalusian?

Not only do they look impressive, but Andalusians are also renowned for being really smart and sensible, too – the perfect combo if you're undertaking advanced training. They're also super-versatile horses, partly because they're naturally short-coupled and balanced, so they find it easy to engage their hindquarters and show off their paces, jump fences, or pirouette handily.

What does it take?

Becoming an equine movie star's a tough job, and trainers know quite early on if a horse has the right temperament. If they do, there are several different ways they can specialise. No horse is ever required to do all the jobs, so he might become...

- **a carriage horse** This might be on his own or as part of a pair or team of horses
- **an actor's horse** The schoolmasters of the stunt world – they can be relied on to behave themselves while inexperienced actors are on board
- **a stunt horse** Some horses are trained to fall safely, with or without a rider, while others can be ridden at speed without tack, or with a trained stunt rider standing on their backs
- **a background horse** The equine version of an extra – he's not the star of the show, but provides extra atmosphere and always behaves himself

DID YOU KNOW?

Stunt horses often enjoy careers well into their 20s because they're so well-pampered – like 26-year-old Rusty, who came to the UK way back in 2000 for the film *Gladiator*. His secret? Lots of time in the field and bimonthly massages! How dreamy!

From film star to five star

Most stunt horses are owned by trainers and stay in the job throughout their careers. But not all... after appearing in the first *Lord of the Rings* film, New Zealand Thoroughbred Frodo Baggins became a successful event horse with US rider Lainey Ashker, even being short-listed for the Olympics!

SHOW RING ready

Get your fave pony looking his best with our guide to creating the perfect plaits

Whether you've never plaited before or you're looking to brush up on your skills, follow our step-by-step guide to creating awesome plaits so your pony can look super-smart every competition day.

STEP ONE

Grab a bucket of water and sponge to wet your pony's mane. Use the wet sponge to bring his mane over to one side and lay it flat. This will make it easier to create neater, tighter plaits because you'll have more grip.

STEP TWO

Use a comb to brush through his mane and remove any knots. Don't be tempted to use a detangling spray because it will make his mane really slippery and tricky to plait.

STEP THREE

Now his mane's tangle-free and sitting neatly, use your comb to divide it into sections. Working along his neck, create evenly sized bunches and secure each one with a plaiting band.

TOP TIP

Is your pony's mane a little wild and in need of a tidy up? Why not ask your yard manager to give it a trim first? It'll make the plaiting process much easier for you if his mane's short and not too thick.

STEP FOUR

Next it's time to begin plaiting! Starting at one end of his neck, remove the plaiting band from the first bunch and split it into three even sections. Plait all the way down to the bottom and, as you reach the end, secure it with a band. On the last round, fold the end of the hair under to create a small loop and secure it in place with another twist of the band.

→

Don't be tempted to use a detangling spray because it will make his mane really slippery

STEP FIVE

Continue to plait along his mane, keeping the sections even and the tightness of your plaits consistent. Paying attention to these details will give you a professional finish.

STEP SIX

Now you've finished the plaits, it's time to roll them up. Grab another band and, taking one plait at a time, fold it in half towards your pony's neck, then fold again so it looks like a ball and secure the band around the rolled plait. Do this to each plait, checking to ensure they're even.

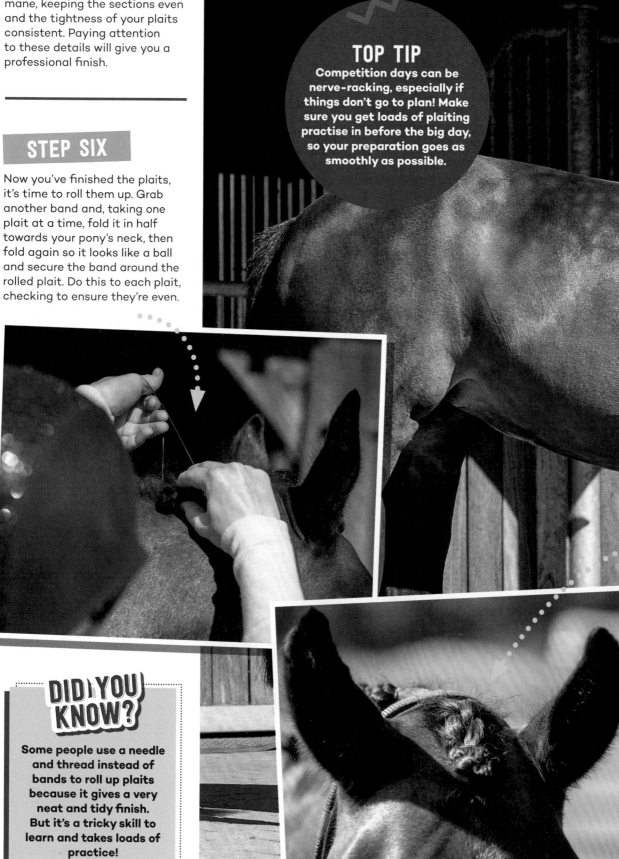

TOP TIP

Competition days can be nerve-racking, especially if things don't go to plan! Make sure you get loads of plaiting practise in before the big day, so your preparation goes as smoothly as possible.

DID YOU KNOW?

Some people use a needle and thread instead of bands to roll up plaits because it gives a very neat and tidy finish. But it's a tricky skill to learn and takes loads of practice!

Plaiting tips

- If it's warm enough, wash your pony's mane the day before you need to plait. Doing this will make his mane really clean and not too slippery to handle.

- The thickness and number (usually 9–13 along his mane plus one in his forelock) of your pony's plaits depends on his type. If he's fine, he'll look smarter with more smaller, dainty plaits, whereas if he's a heavier breed, he'll usually suit fewer, chunkier ones.

- To make your rolled-up plaits really secure, add an extra band in case one breaks, or have a go at using a needle and thread if you're feeling confident!

- Plaiting sprays can be really handy because they'll provide the perfect grip so you can create the neatest plaits around. These sprays also give his mane a shiny finish.

STEP SEVEN

Last but not least, his forelock! You can either plait it in the same way as his mane, or you can do a French plait – which will look sooo fancy! To do this, split the top of the forelock into three bunches and add in an extra section on each side as you plait down. Secure the plait with a band, roll it up and there you have it – a super-smart pony, ready for the show ring!

RACES

Looking to add even more fun to your riding lesson or schooling session? Here are 10 ace games to play with ponies and pals!

Egg and spoon

Grab a spoon and pop an egg or soft ball on top and off you go, stopping the timer as you cross the finish line. The quickest time wins – careful not to drop your egg, though, or you'll waste time picking it up!

Chase me, Charlie

Feeling confident and up for a jumping challenge? In a game of Chase me, Charlie the height of the jump increases every round. If your pony refuses or knocks a pole, you're out. The combination who jumps the biggest fence clear, wins!

Traffic lights

Each traffic light colour is a different pace, for example...
- ⬤ **Red**'s halt
- ◯ **Amber**'s walk
- ◯ **Green**'s trot

Ask your instructor to call out colours. If you make a wrong move, you'll get faults! The winner is the person with the fewest faults at the end.

TOP TIP

Why not add another element to some of the races and relay with your pony? Ask a friend to hold him at the start line and have a go on foot, too!

Slalom

Place two sets of four wings or blocks in a straight line down the middle of the arena and weave in and out of them as you race against your pals. Then turn around at the end and go back through the slalom. Start out in walk to build up your confidence, then have a go in trot – the quickest wins!

Block elimination

Set up five or six blocks in a row. Take it in turns to jump the blocks, aiming for the middle and removing one block after every round. This game gets super-tricky and will definitely test your pony's straightness!

Grandma's footsteps

Time to check out your pony's responsiveness! Starting at one end of the arena, get your pals to line up and ask your instructor to stand at the other end. While she's facing away from you, make your way towards her – but when she turns around, halt quickly! If she catches you moving, you'll be out. The person who reaches her first wins!

Through the paces

This game's super-simple! All you have to do is set out two cones, one at each end of the arena, then race against your friend, walking for the first leg, trotting for the second and cantering the last. If you accidentally break into a faster pace, you'll have to turn your pony in a circle as a penalty!

Musical markers

Play your fave songs and ride around the arena until the music stops, then head straight for a marker or cone. Make sure there's one less cone than there are riders. Every person who reaches a cone scores one point. After 10 rounds, count up your points to see who's come out on top!

WEB EXTRA
For more fun games and demo videos, visit...
bit.ly/WACKY_RACES

HOW TO RIDE A...
LAZY PONY

Give your pony a boost with our tips for getting him going forwards

We've all ridden a pony who won't move off our leg. It might give you a good workout, but teaching him to listen to your aids and think forwards is the key to improving his schooling, jumping and overall rideability. Here's how!

1. OFF THE LEG

Transitions are a great way to teach your pony to be more attentive to your aids. They'll get him listening closely and will help him think forwards, no matter whether you're doing flatwork or jumping. They'll build his strength, too, which will help make him feel more confident about going forwards.

TOP TIP

If your pony doesn't move forward when you squeeze with your legs, give him one firmer leg aid then a tap with the whip to help him learn that he needs to go forward straight away.

2. SKY HIGH

If your pony enjoys it, why not use small fences and poles to encourage him forwards during your flatwork sessions? They won't make your dressage worse – in fact, they could improve it. They'll make your session way more fun, too!

3. OUT AND ABOUT

A really good solution for slower ponies is lots of hacking. It's really fun for him and you can even do your schooling out on a hack! Leg-yield, bending exercises and transitions are all achievable on bridleways, so there's you can ditch the school and get out on the tracks – even if not every day! Like transitions, it'll make him stronger, too.

TOP TIP
You could take your schooling sessions into an empty field to give your pony a boost.

4. WHAT DOES HE LOVE?

Think about what your pony enjoys, because if he's unhappy with what you're asking he probably won't be very enthusiastic, which can make him slower. If he loves fast hacks and raised polework, can you add more sessions into his routine? If sessions full of circles and serpentines switch off his brain, avoid them and try something new.

5. PAIN, PAIN, GO AWAY

If your pony's sore, it can make him more reluctant to move forward. So, it's super-important to get your vet out to check him over and make sure he's comfortable. Look out for whether he feels the same on both reins, and in walk, trot and canter. Your vet will be able to tell you whether he could be uncomfortable, but get his back, tack and teeth checked, too, just in case.

7. FULL TUMMY

Is your pony getting enough to eat? Could he benefit from a higher energy diet to give him a boost without the added calories? Speak to a qualified nutritionist who'll let you know if a change to his diet could help. Often, ponies who need a low-calorie diet to maintain their weight can be a bit less forward-going, so thinking about how you can feed him for energy without added weight is important.

6. BACK TO SCHOOL

It could be that your pony just doesn't understand what you're asking. If this is the case, take things back to basics and make sure he knows that leg means he needs to go forwards. Use your voice and a tap with the whip to help him associate your leg aids with going forwards.

SUMMER ✓ CHECKLIST

Make sure your pony's in perfect health during the summer season

Summer's one of the best times for ponies because there's no mud and a tonne of fun activities you can do together! But there are some specific things you need to keep on top of, too, to make sure he stays super-happy and healthy. Use our handy checklist to help.

☐ Watch his weight

Sugary spring and summer grass means your pony may be munching a few too many calories while he's out in the field! It's extra-important to monitor his weight over the summer months so you can detect any changes early on.
Do this by...

- **weightaping** Use the same weightape each week – wrap it around his middle and write down his weight to help you keep track of any changes

- **condition scoring** This clever technique means looking at and feeling your pony's body to assess how much muscle and fat he has. It takes practice, so ask your instructor or yard owner to explain how to do it – or follow our handy PONY guide at **bit.ly/CONDITION_GUIDE**

- **weighbridge** This is the most accurate way to find out your pony's weight. Lots of vet practices have them, or you can book an equine nutritionist to visit your yard and bring one

☐ Look for lami

Did you know that 10% of ponies get laminitis every year? If your pony's had it before, it's important to be extra vigilant, but even if not it's still a good idea to know the signs and keep an eye out for them...
- watch him moving around – is he moving normally?
- feel his hooves – are they warmer than usual? One or two really hot hooves can be a tell-tale sign
- ask an experienced adult to find and check his digital pulse – a high one could signal a problem
- check his heart rate using a stethoscope – if it's higher than normal he may be in pain

Keep an eye out

Your pony's eyes are super-delicate and a magnet for flies, which can really irritate him and cause problems. If he's bothered by them, consider fitting him with a fly mask or fringe to keep the pests away! Check his eyes every day – use damp cotton wool to remove any discharge from the corners, but never touch your pony's eye. Pale cream or clear discharge is common, but if it's yellow or green, it's a sign of infection and a vet visit's in order.

TOP TIP
If you think there might be something wrong with either of your pony's eyes, call the vet as soon as possible.

DID YOU KNOW?
A key sign that your pony has a problem with his teeth is quidding, which is when he drops food out of his mouth when he eats.

Tooth check

Your pony's teeth need to be checked by your vet or a qualified equine dental technician at least every year. But between visits, it's a good idea to keep an eye on his teeth so you can pick up on any problems early on.

Either as part of your grooming or tacking up routine, each week gently open his lips to reveal his front teeth. Look for any chips to his teeth, and cuts or ulcers on his gums.

Early bird catches the worm

Every pony needs to be checked and treated for worms depending on the season. In the spring and summer months, you can keep track of his worm burden by carrying out regular worm egg counts (WECs) and then, if his number's too high, your vet will advise how to treat it using a targeted wormer.

FESS UPS

Get ready to giggle at these goofy ponies' confessions!

WIDE LOAD

Lisa, my rider, keeps feeding me loads of apples. They're my fave treat, so I just can't resist – even if I'm full to the brim with grass! She keeps feeding me more and more, and these extra snacks have made me a little wider than I'd normally be at this time of year. Anyway, going cross-country's my absolute fave activity and as we were schooling today I cantered up to a really skinny fence with flags either side. I nailed the perfect stride but because I'm so wide, Lisa's toes knocked both flags over! It was sooo embarrassing, I've got to go on a diet – I'll never eat an apple again! Or maybe just until next week...

Gloria

DREAM A LITTLE DREAM

This morning I stood up and shook the straw off my back. It was the best sleep of my entire life – I was dreaming for hours! I'd dreamt about galloping through a grassy field with my best friend, Tiny. We then had a contest to see who could whinny the loudest – I won, obvs.

In the field this afternoon, Tiny galloped up to me giggling. He'd been spying on my owner, Izzy, who was showing all her friends a video on her phone. She'd filmed me sleeping! Well, not just sleeping... snoring and whinnying in my sleep!

Twizzle

BLAST OFF!

Surprisingly, Will and I were having a great dressage lesson. Jumping's our fave, but his mum insisted we improve our flatwork skills, too. We'd been working on getting more impulsion in my canter and the instructor asked Will to give the lengthening exercise one last go. It was the end of the lesson, so I was pretty tired. But off we went, cantering around the arena. In the corner, Will kicked me on and out of nowhere, a bird flew out straight into my bottom! I went really fast to run away! Maybe that was the trick to lengthening my stride... LOL!

Batman

FRIGHTFULLY COLD

I cantered along the beach having so much fun with my owner, Sam. I don't like water much, but I was feeling so brave I even dipped my hooves into the sea. My bestie Eddie and his owner, Jessie, were so confident – they were splashing loads. I'll admit I was jealous, so I needed to take the plunge. With Sam's guidance I walked into the water and it slowly rose above my knees. Suddenly, a big wave came and the water touched my belly – it was sooo cold. It totally shocked me and I pooped a bit! I turned around to see it floating. Then it washed up onto the beach where loads of people were sitting – whoops!

Chico

SHAKE IT OFF

I love a good roll in the dustiest patch of the field. One sunny Sunday, Meg was giving me a bath. It was a hot day, so I was happy to be cooled down! Meg always stands in a funny position so the water doesn't run down her arms. I've got no idea why she wouldn't want to get wet, especially on a day like today – it's sooo refreshing! So, I decided to take matters into my own hooves. When I was completely soaked, I did a full body shake so Meg could be nice and cool, too. Weirdly, she didn't seem happy about it. Oopsie!

Delilah

CRINGE-O-METER

Waaay cringe!   Wasn't me!   Kinda cringe!

ACCURACY IS KEY

When I need the toilet, I have to stop. None of this trotting and pooing business! But today I totally embarrassed myself. In the middle of our dressage test, I had a sudden panic. I felt my tummy rumble, 'oh no, not now!' I thought. As we came back to walk at H, I was praying we'd do a halt transition soon. Luck was on my side, and we halted at C. I couldn't hold it in any longer. Hey – at least I timed it well, we were in halt already! I looked up, listening to Lily's aids and noticed we were right in front of the judges. Oops! Lily rolled her eyes and we completed the test – hopefully I didn't lose us any marks!

Bobby

STEAL THE SHOW

Do you have the cutest pony ever? Find out all about how to show him

Showing is something that so many ponies can do well at because there are tonnes of classes to choose from! From working hunter, mountain and moorland and even pony judge would most like to take home, we can guarantee there'll be a class for you! To help you know where to start, we've got the lowdown on all things showing.

DID YOU KNOW?

It can give your pony's appearance a boost if you give him gorgeous plaits, however for mountain & moorland classes, you should leave his mane and tail natural and flowing.

Time to shine

There are loads of shows that happen all over the UK, from local fun ones with novelty classes, such as fancy dress and handsomest gelding, to county competitions with qualifiers for prestigious championships, such as Horse of the Year Show and more. Whatever your level, why not give it a go? You'll need to make sure your pony's groomed to perfection on the day with pristine tack and perfect plaits, and that he's in excellent general condition.

Which one?

Different classes have different requirements, so do a bit of research to see which one your pony might suit best. For example, if he's a stunning appaloosa, a rare breeds class may work best. A golden oldie? Why not enter him into a class for veterans? The list is endless!

Follow the leader

You don't have to ride to do showing! If you own a super-cute miniature or a retired pony, in-hand showing may be just the thing. You can give in-hand showing a try with any type of pony, but you'll need to make sure you have full control over him and be confident to trot him in-hand. He'll also need to be able to stand still for long enough without fidgeting or trying to eat the grass while the judge does their inspection!

What do you have to do?

In most ridden showing classes, this is what you can expect...

1. All the riders and ponies will walk round in open order. Keep at least one pony's distance between you at all times, and find a gap or circle if you get too close.
2. You'll then be asked to trot, and sometimes canter, all together, before making a change of rein and doing the same thing the other way. While you do this, the judge will be watching.
3. The judge will call you in to line up and inspect each pony individually.
4. You'll then ride your individual show in trot and canter around the arena, perhaps riding a figure-of-eight to change rein. This is the time to really show off your pony's paces!
5. Once everyone's been, you'll walk large again and the judge will announce the final placings.

TOP TIP

All judges have their own likes and dislikes, so don't be too disheartened if you don't get a good result one day!

DID YOU KNOW?

In affiliated ridden classes, your pony will be ridden by the judge, too!

Step it up

If you want a little extra thrill, a working hunter pony class could be just right! Alongside judging all the regular things, such as turnout and conformation, the judge will also watch you and your pony jump a course of rustic fences. The height of the fences will depend on the level you enter, and there are even lead rein classes for mini working hunters!

THE FIRST PONY IN SPACE

Freddie and Astro embark on a space-tacular adventure in the year 2123

Ever since Freddie was small, he'd been obsessed with space. He used to daydream about flying a rocketship all the way to Mars, and beyond. However, his space dreams were on hold for now because he had an earthly passion, too – ponies. Freddie thought galloping as fast as he could on a pony was the closest he could get to lift-off in a rocketship. He loved nothing more than zooming over fences and riding on thrilling hacks across the countryside. Eventually, Freddie's parents decided he was ready to have a pony of his own, and that's when they bought a 146cm Thoroughbred X, who Freddie named Astro.

In the running

Freddie was part of the Northtown Pony Club and he absolutely loved racing Astro against his friends. She was incredibly fast and, so far, the pair held the record speed in the local area for pony racing. It had earned them a place in the Pony Racing Championships and, for Freddie, there was a lot more riding on their result than just a red rosette. It would determine who'd be selected to compete for their country, and take part in the first-ever pony race on the moon!

Freddie's stomach churned as he queued at the start line, while Astro pawed the ground in anticipation. "On your marks," the race starter said into the jockeys' earpieces. "Get set," Freddie checked his goggles were in place. "Go!" They were off, and Freddie and Astro knew what they had to do. The other ponies were fast, but Freddie didn't mind Astro conserving her energy until the last stretch. She surged past the group, edging close to the combination currently in first place. Approaching the finish line, Freddie gave her a squeeze and Astro lowered, becoming totally streamlined. As they crossed the finish, she was a nose ahead. Freddie threw his arms around her neck as the tannoy announced that they'd won. He couldn't believe it. "And keep your eyes on this pair, folks. Frederick and Astronomical

Discovery – aptly named – will be representing the UK in the first-ever pony race in space!"

Vital prep

In the months that followed, Freddie and Astro had to undergo rigorous health checks and tests to prove they could handle going to space. They practised in anti-gravity chambers and were each fitted with custom-made spacesuits. The equine version was a brand-new prototype that'd been designed to allow the horses to run at full capacity, with their sweat absorbed from and released into the atmosphere. NASA had designed special hoof boots, too, with the optimum amount of gravity boost, to replicate levels on Earth while they galloped across the moon's surface.

The rocketship that the ponies would fly up in had special equine chambers, kitted out with a supply of vacuum-packed hay and water, which would be their home for the duration of the three-day journey.

Up in a rocket

Launch day finally arrived and Freddie was totally buzzing, but also a little nervous. He hoped Astro would travel well, and was confident their training had prepared her. When the time came to let the grooms load Astro onto the rocket, he gave her a kiss on the nose. "See you on the other side," he whispered. As he watched her head towards the ramp with the other racing ponies, Freddie wiped away a stray tear and went with his parents to take his position in the rocket.

Everyone's spacesuits were on, and Freddie had to pinch himself to believe his dream of space – along with his love of ponies – had got him to this amazing point. He took his seat next to his mum and

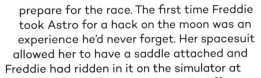

felt like he was in a dream. When the countdown for lift-off started, Freddie knew this would be the beginning of an epic adventure.

One small step for ponykind

The three days that followed were like nothing Freddie had ever experienced. He was given a tablet to view Astro the whole time in her stable and, as he knew she would be, she remained cool, calm and content the whole time. Freddie was loving being in a real-life rocket, and the dehydrated space food actually wasn't bad! The view out of the window was absolutely incredible as they powered away from Earth – it looked so enormous to begin with, but with each day that passed it got smaller and smaller.

When they touched down on the moon, Freddie was unbelievably excited. He was really there, in space! But all he wanted to do was see Astro. The United Kingdom had won the right to have its pony be the first to step onto the moon – and that was Astro! Her name would go into the history books. The grooms helped Freddie unload her. She was in her spacesuit, which was the coolest thing Freddie had ever seen. He helped lead Astro onto the surface of the moon and into a corral. A camera flashed as they posed for a picture that was instantly beamed to every newsroom around the world.

Getting acclimatised

Astro and Freddie had a week to acclimatise to this alien environment. Astro and the other racing ponies were stabled in a giant space barn, where they were able to have their suits removed and live practically normally. The barn had gravity and oxygen, and there was an adjoining indoor school where the jockeys could exercise the horses. However, it was important that they trained on the moon's surface, too, to

> **The first time Freddie took Astro for a hack on the moon was an experience he'd never forget**

prepare for the race. The first time Freddie took Astro for a hack on the moon was an experience he'd never forget. Her spacesuit allowed her to have a saddle attached and Freddie had ridden in it on the simulator at home, but doing it for real was totally different. Freddie went with the Thai rider and his pony, and they meandered around the craters and past the space station.

The racetrack had been designed specially, and a huge vehicle had rolled a smooth path for the horses to gallop along. The cushioning in their hoof boots meant that they could run on any surface, and the zero-gravity atmosphere gave everything a little extra bounce. Astro felt on top form when they did a practice run the day before the race and Freddie couldn't wait for it to take place. Just being there was an immense feeling, and he couldn't even begin to contemplate how he'd feel if they actually won.

The space race

Race day felt strange because there were no huge crowds like at a usual pony race, just the parents of each child competing, watching in their spacesuits from the sidelines. The whole thing was being televised live back on Earth, and Freddie couldn't imagine how many people would be watching, including all his friends and family.

The jockeys rode to the start line, about to make history. Freddie's Thai friend gave him a little wave. Riding in spacesuits felt a bit crunchy and bulky, but by now everyone was used to them.

This was it. The moment they'd all been waiting for. The jockeys' earpieces rang in unison to signal the start of the race. All Freddie could hear was blood rushing in his ears as Astro surged forward. She charged to the front of the group – it was as if she was born for this moment. Freddie felt his nerves bubbling up – this was so unlike Astro, she always hung back and let the other ponies do the hard work of leading the race, then came from behind to take the lead late-on. But Astro didn't tire, and seemed to be using the bounce of zero gravity to elongate her stride even more. She won by five lengths and, as they slowed up after the finish line, all Freddie could hear in his earpiece was cheering. Every pony and rider finished safely – the Russian pair in second, Australian third and his new friend from Thailand in sixth. Freddie and Astro would go down in history as the winners of the first pony race on the moon. Now, he couldn't wait to get back to Earth for their next chapter.

AWESOME Adventures

What's better than an epic hack with your fave pony?

Not only is hacking the perfect time for a catch-up with your yard mates, but it's also great fun for your fave pony. Regular hacks will mentally stimulate him, boosting his happiness. Plus, enjoying a fun adventure together is sure to make you feel good and improve your bond.

1

Which way?
Before you head out on your next adventure, plan the route you're going to take. It's a good idea to work out how far you're going and how long you'll be out for so you can let your yard manager or a parent know. If the ground isn't too hard, or slippy, and you're feeling confident plan a long canter into your hack — it's sure to give you a buzz!

2

All aboard!
It's important to be able to mount and dismount from the ground. If you've ever dropped your whip or struggled to open a gate, you'll know why! Spend some time teaching your pony to stand quietly, and practising mounting from the ground as well as a block, too.

3

In the know

Wearing the correct safety gear is essential. This includes an up-to-standard riding hat, body protector and plenty of high-vis on you and your pony. Make sure your high-vis can be seen from all angles and aim to wear a mixture of colours so you really stand out – you can never be too safe! Make sure you're familiar with the Highway Code, too. From road signs to arm and hand signals, it's really important that you know the rules to help keep you and your pony safe.

4

Stable mates

Hacking with pals is super-fun and, unlike in your lessons, you'll get the chance to talk all things pony along the way and plan your next sleepover or comp! Why not organise a group hack with your pals to celebrate something? It could be a birthday or the start of school holidays!

5 Must-have manners

Having a polite pony makes handling him sooo much easier. Plus, it makes your hacking way more enjoyable. He should always stop when you ask and stand patiently – you might need to cross a road or wait for a gate to be opened. Why not practise your halt transitions when schooling him to test your aids?

6 Mix 'n' match

If possible, avoid doing the same route every time you go out. Your pony might get bored and he'll quickly learn where he can go faster. Try hacking on the roads or in woodlands and open spaces to mix it up – he's sure to become more bold as he sees different places.

7 Through the paces

Loads of riders use hacking to build fitness. This doesn't mean you have to canter or gallop every time, his fitness will still increase from a long walk! Be sure to check the ground before you do any fast work, though.

Did you know, hacking could boost your dressage scores, too? Try practising some of your flatwork moves out hacking and you're sure to see a difference. Plus, your pals will be totally impressed if you start leg-yielding along a bridlepath!

8 Routine ready

If your pony's lazy in the school or gets bored quickly, try taking him for a short hack to warm up before you head into the arena. It'll wake him up so he's ready to turn his hoof to anything you ask. Going for a wander after your session to cool down is so much nicer than walking around the arena, too.

9 New scenes

If there's a lack of hacking options at your yard, why not take a trip somewhere different? There's sure to be endless choices of places to go nearby – maybe the beach or a famous park. Be sure to check their rules and regs for horse riding first, though.

10 Deeper connection

Hacking's meant to be exciting and fun, but it can be nerve-wracking riding a pony you don't know too well. You'll deffo build a stronger bond if you go adventuring and you'll gain heaps of confidence, too. Plus, it's also the perfect time to chat to your pony and tell him any of your worries. He's a great listener and you'll feel loads better after you've had a awesome ride in the countryside.

A DAY IN the life

Find out how Abby and Helena care for their ponies around school

Having a great routine to help you take care of your fave pony in between school and homework is really important because it'll give you more time for having fun with him. So, check out how Abby and Helena take care of yard duties and look after their ponies!

TOP TIP

It's really important to check on ponies who live out full-time to make su they don't have any injuri pick out their feet and adjust rugs to prevent them from rubbing.

BEFORE SCHOOL

7am First, we feed the ponies who are stabled overnight – Eddie and Star.

7.15am Next, it's time to check the ponies out in the field and change their rugs. Helena's pony Willow and our retired pony Sandy live out 24/7.

TOP TIP

Sharing duties on the yard with your friends will get everything done more quickly and leave you with more time for adventures!

7.30am We swap Eddie and Star's rugs and turn them out in their fields.

7.45am Before we go to school, we make up feeds for the evening and next morning, and fill some haynets to put in the steamer for later.

8am Time to go to school. We can't wait to see the ponies when we get home!

AFTER SCHOOL

TOP TIP
Use your broom to clear any cobwebs in your pony's stable while you muck out.

4.30pm As soon as we get back we change into jodhpurs and boots, grab a wheelbarrow and start mucking out Eddie and Star's stables. Today we put in a new bag of bedding.

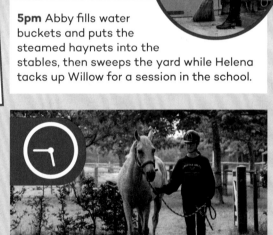

5pm Abby fills water buckets and puts the steamed haynets into the stables, then sweeps the yard while Helena tacks up Willow for a session in the school.

5.15pm Abby helps Helena ride in the school, setting out poles and giving her pointers when she needs them.

5.45pm It's time for Eddie and Star to come in for the night. We turn Willow out and check on Sandy, then, bring in Eddie and Star, and give them their dinners.

6pm Time to say goodnight! We give the ponies a big cuddle, then head home for homework and dinner.

WHICH MYSTICAL PONY ARE YOU?

Take our fun quiz to find out which type of mythical equine matches your personality

Pegasus

Like perfect Pegasus, your dreams know no bounds. Pegasus spends most of his time flying through the sky, and similarly you have a tendency to daydream with your head in the clouds! Air is your element, and this makes you imaginative, optimistic and funny, too. You enchant everyone you meet, and can achieve anything you put your mind to.

Unicorn

Unicorn is one of the most magical creatures of all and acts as the guardian of the animal kingdom. Like her, you're a really caring person and always put others before yourself. Earth is your element, which makes you grounded and empathic. This means you love nothing more than grooming and pampering your fave pony, and to show how much you love her.

Lesson for sure!

Would you rather have a lesson with your fave instructor, or take your pony out competing?

QUITE SHY

START

Are you quite shy or more outgoing?

Long and flowing

How do you prefer a pony's mane to look

OUTGOING

Definitely riding

What's the best thing about owning a pony

What's your fave pace?

Taking care of him

A smooth, stready trot

Jumping

Hacking

Which activity's your fave?

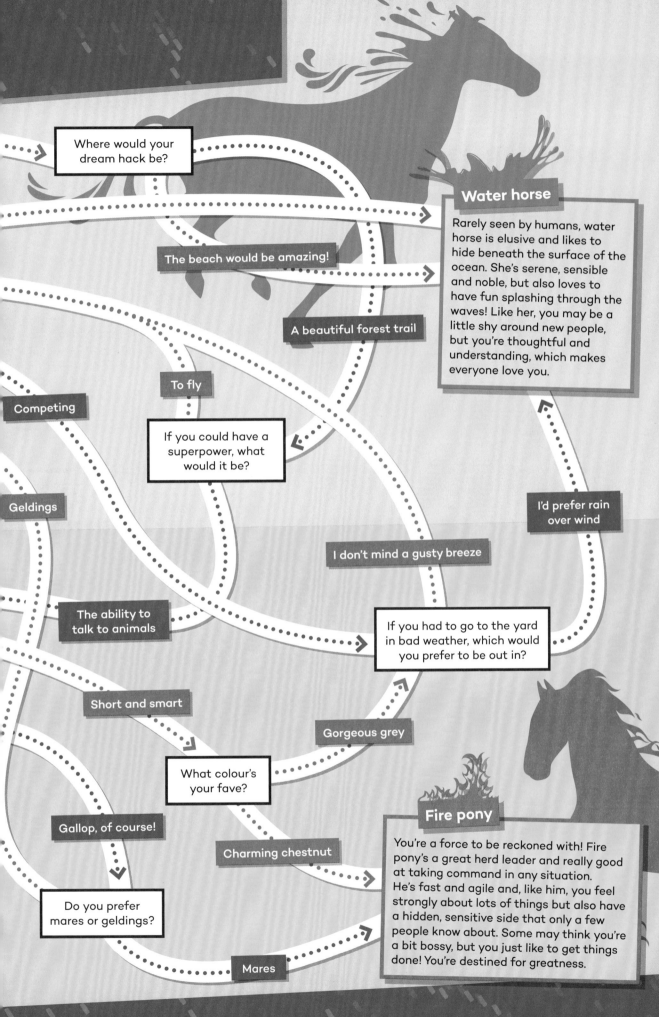

Where would your dream hack be?

The beach would be amazing!

A beautiful forest trail

Water horse

Rarely seen by humans, water horse is elusive and likes to hide beneath the surface of the ocean. She's serene, sensible and noble, but also loves to have fun splashing through the waves! Like her, you may be a little shy around new people, but you're thoughtful and understanding, which makes everyone love you.

To fly

Competing

If you could have a superpower, what would it be?

Geldings

I'd prefer rain over wind

I don't mind a gusty breeze

The ability to talk to animals

If you had to go to the yard in bad weather, which would you prefer to be out in?

Short and smart

Gorgeous grey

What colour's your fave?

Fire pony

You're a force to be reckoned with! Fire pony's a great herd leader and really good at taking command in any situation. He's fast and agile and, like him, you feel strongly about lots of things but also have a hidden, sensitive side that only a few people know about. Some may think you're a bit bossy, but you just like to get things done! You're destined for greatness.

Gallop, of course!

Charming chestnut

Do you prefer mares or geldings?

Mares

BECOMING US

Get to know your fave pony so you can be best friends for life

Building an unbreakable bond with your equine friend – whether you own, share or ride him in your weekly lessons – means you can get the most out of your time together and have hours of fun, no matter what you decide to do. Check out all the ways to learn more about your fave pony and how you can become besties.

TOP TIP
Why not make a note of all the things you learn about your favourite pony? Doing this will help you track his wellbeing and means you might be able to recognise patterns in his behaviour.

Quiz master
Whether it's the instructor at your riding school, his old owner or another person who rides him, the quickest way to learn loads about your fave pony is by asking the people who know him best lots of questions! You could ask them...
- how old is he?
- does he prefer schooling or hacking?
- is he slow, spooky or speedy?
- does he bang on the door at feed time?
- what breed is he?
- does he prefer to live out at night?

Particular taste
You'll quickly become best friends with your pony if you get to know his likes and dislikes. By knowing what his fave things are, you can avoid wasting time by doing things that don't make him happy and spend more time doing what he loves.

Get to know your pony's good and bad habits, too. Does he try to barge out the stable door as soon as you open it? Or does he drag you to the same spot of lush grass on his way to the field? Learning about his naughty habits means you can handle him with confidence and finding out if he has any cute or funny habits means you can capture them on camera!

Get a feel

Becoming familiar with each part of your pony's body, from his ears right down to his hooves, will help you to quickly identify any problems that might arise, such as cuts, swollen areas or unexpected weight loss. It's a good idea to check him over every time you see him and take his temperature, pulse and respiration regularly, so you know what's normal for him. Weightaping and body condition scoring him every other week is really useful, too, whether you're trying to slim him down or want him to maintain peak condition.

TOP TIP

Always make any changes to your pony's diet or management routine slowly to give him plenty of time to adjust.

Trying new activities will help you understand more about your pony's personality

At one with nature

Sitting near your pony's field and observing him while he grazes and interacts with his herdmates isn't only a peaceful pastime, it'll teach you how he acts around other ponies and what he enjoys doing most, too. Maybe food is his priority and he's happy to graze away from the herd, or perhaps he needs his friends to feel secure and prefers to stay close. Either way, watching him hang out with pals will help you discover loads about pony behaviour.

DID YOU KNOW?

Ponies are very sociable animals and, in the wild, they live in big herds. To strengthen their bond with their herdmates, they spend time grooming and playing with each other – similar to how you'll get to know him best, too!

Watch and learn

Keep a beady eye on your pony while other people handle him so you can see how he reacts with different people. Is he super-friendly and eager to get everyone's attention? Or does he shy away when a new person handles him? Knowing his reactions means you can be ready to tackle situations he finds nerve-racking or exciting. If the pony in question is your own, try to attend farrier and vet visits, too, so you can see how he behaves then, too.

Taster session

Trying new activities will help you understand more about your pony's personality. Is he really brave and does he tackle new adventures with confidence? Or is he wary about situations or places he's never been before? Knowing how he's likely to react will allow you to prepare ahead of time and manage him so he stays calm, relaxed and happy.

Slow and steady

It's super-important to take your time getting to know a new pony. Don't rush to try everything at once because you might knock your confidence. If you're feeling unsure, it's okay to take a step back and try again another time. Enjoying your time together means you'll build on your relationship and have even more good times!

TOP TIP

If your pony's the nervous type, why not bring along his best equine pal to try some new activities? They'll help give him tonnes of confidence, which means you won't feel as worried or restricted when it comes to having a go at something new.

Hours on end

In short, putting in the hours will help you get to know your pony better. Whatever you do to learn more about him, whether it's pampering or cuddling him, taking him for a graze in-hand or just chilling together in his stable, it'll be time well spent and, as a result, you'll be able to enjoy heaps more epic adventures.

MOSAIC HORSESHOES

Make

Create your own lucky horseshoe with our cute make

Looking for a homemade lucky charm for all your riding adventures? Here's how to make and decorate a saltdough horseshoe!

You'll need

- ✓ 150g plain flour
- ✓ 75g salt
- ✓ 75ml water
- ✓ mosaic tiles
- ✓ PVA glue
- ✓ string or ribbon

TOP TIP
Why not make some adorable Christmas decorations using the same method? Just use red, green or gold materials to nail the festive vibe!

Let's get started...

1 Weigh out all your ingredients and mix the flour and salt in a bowl.

2 Add in the water, then combine until it forms a smooth dough.

3 Place the saltdough on a lightly floured surface and roll out until about 1cm thick.

4 Carefully cut out a horseshoe shape. You can use a cookie cutter or cut round a template if you prefer!

5 Place your horseshoe onto a baking tray lined with greaseproof paper. Then, use a chopstick to make a hole on each side of the top of your shoe so you can hang it up later on.

6 Bake the horseshoes in a preheated oven set to its lowest temperature (around 40°C if possible) for four hours, or until completely dry and solid.

7 Once baked, use your PVA glue to stick on the mosaic tiles around the horseshoe.

TOP TIP
Why not have a go at making lots of different shapes with your saltdough? You could do a pony portrait or cut out letters to make your pony's name!

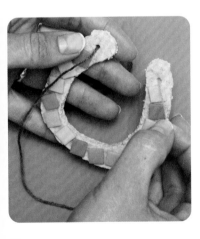

8 When the glue's dried, thread your string through the holes and there you have it – one super-cute lucky horseshoe!

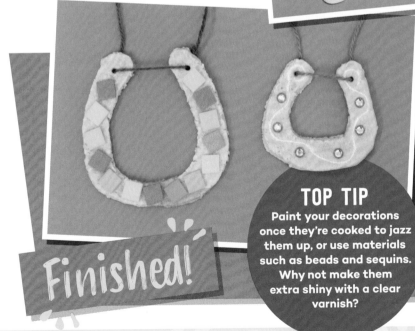

Finished!

TOP TIP
Paint your decorations once they're cooked to jazz them up, or use materials such as beads and sequins. Why not make them extra shiny with a clear varnish?

THE SHIRE

They might have been bred for hard work on the farm, but these days you're more likely to spot the impressive Shire horse on royal duties

Whether you've watched the Household Cavalry in action on Horse Guards Parade in St James Park or on display at the London International Horse Show, you've seen how impeccably trained these remarkable horses are. They're so impressive because they perform complicated drill manoeuvres without missing a beat and are often watched over by Her Majesty the Queen herself – talk about pressure! Here's everything you need to know about these talented giants.

DID YOU KNOW?

A Shire horse called Sampson holds the record for being the tallest horse ever. He was born in 1846 and measured a massive 21.2 1/2 hands – that's 2.19m!

How to spot them

Though some reach dizzying heights at 19hh, the average for a Shire horse is around 17.2hh. They're exceptionally strong, but elegant for their size and strength with pretty, kind-eyed heads, slightly arched necks, and short backs that make them look almost like a heavy sport horse. They also have silky feathers, often paired with white markings on their legs – so you know someone is busy with the purple shampoo behind the scenes!

Why the Shire?

There are several British draft breeds who can become drum horses in the Household Cavalry, but the Shire is particularly special because it's endangered, and showing off for packed crowds is a great opportunity to demonstrate how cool Shires are. They're also renowned for their level-headed temperaments, which is super-important when it comes to participating in royal ceremonies in front of thousands of people. Their strength is also really important, because ceremonial kit is heavy – a drum horse has to carry up to 18 stone!

What does it take?

Finding suitable horses is really hard, so special buyers visit farms and auctions to try to find young horses who fit the part. Once selected, the suitable candidate will head to a yard in Leicestershire for six weeks to make sure he doesn't have any viruses that might make the other horses unwell. After that, it's time to go to Windsor for training, which begins in-hand and progresses slowly from there, with lots of desensitisation along the way so he's used to loud noises and unexpected sights. It usually takes eight months to a year to prepare him for his debut.

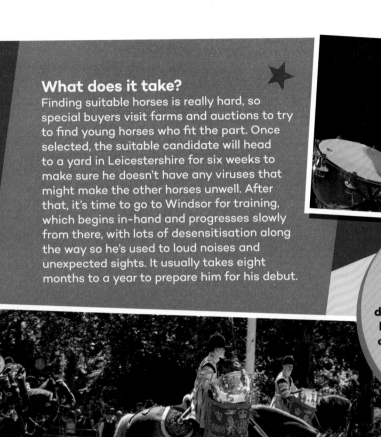

DID YOU KNOW?

If you're riding a drum horse, both of your hands will be busy playing the drums. So, to ensure riders still have control, the reins will be attached to the stirrups. See, using your leg really is the answer to everything!

A piece of history

Heavy horses were the favoured mounts of the cavalry up until the reign of Henry VIII, when the rise of gunpowder meant horses weren't needed in battle. Instead, they were relocated to farms, and when Dutch engineers came over in the 1500s, their Friesian horses were crossed with the native British heavy horses to create a more refined, flashy type.

HOW TO RIDE A...
TENSE PONY

Tense or excited ponies can be super-challenging, so we're here to help you get it right!

Whether he's nervous, excited or won't focus, tense ponies can be a tough type to get the best from. We've put together some top tips to help you ride tense ponies as well as possible and make sure you have loads of fun together.

TOP TIP
Try to keep changing up the exercises you use so your pony doesn't begin to expect them, which will make them less effective for regaining his attention.

1.

SPIN ME ROUND
Circles and bending are perfect for focusing a tense pony, because he'll have to soften and bend through his body. Try not to pull, because he may resist and become more tense. Instead, use gentle squeezes down the rein to ask him to bend. It'll give him something to think about, too, which is super-handy!

2.
EXTRA EXERCISE
Use transitions to improve your pony's focus and encourage him to relax – the busier you keep him and the more simple questions you ask, the more relaxed he'll feel. Keep your hands soft and use your legs to gently support him.

3.
WHAT'S THE PROBLEM?
Try to think about why your pony's struggling to relax. Is he stressed about something in his routine or environment? Does he have too much energy, or does he feel excited? By knowing why he acts the way he does, you'll be in a much better position to figure out how to solve it!

4.
CALM DOWN
Staying calm will help your pony – he can feel if your muscles are tense, which will make him feel more tense, too. Keep your shoulders up and core strong, though, because this will keep you secure in the saddle. Your pony loves to hear your voice, so talk to him gently, or even try singing him a song to help you both chill a bit.
Keep your hands soft and your legs gently hugging his sides. Try to rise slowly in trot and sit deep in walk and canter, too.

5.
FULL OF FEED
Could your pony be getting too much hard feed, or might there be an ingredient that doesn't agree with him? Ask a qualified nutritionist to help you find the perfect diet for him. You could even try a calming supplement, too, but check with your vet that none of the ingredients could stop you being able to compete.

TOP TIP
Make a kit list for show days to help make sure you've got everything packed and ready ahead of time.

6.
UP THE CHALLENGE
Find new ways to challenge yourselves that don't involve things that could stress you or your pony out. Could you add more fillers or extra fences to your grid, or is there a new dressage move you've been wanting to try? Pushing yourselves is the best way to improve, but it's supposed to be fun – and safe, too!

7.
TIME OUT
Leave as much time as possible to make sure you don't feel stressed on show day, or when you go for lessons or clinics. Feeling rushed will only make you – and, by extension, your pony – tense and unhappy. Instead, a stress-free day all comes down to being organised and ahead of the game.

"It's up to you which tasty treat you use, but a lick may help encourage him to hold the stretch for a bit longer"

HOME STRETCH

Supple up your pony from the ground with these fun stretches

Nearly all ponies have one side that's stronger than the other – just like people are left- or right-handed. But with time and training you can help build up your pony's muscles evenly, which will make riding a lot easier for him – and you! So, to help improve his flexibility from the floor, have a go at our super stretch ideas!

Loosen up

There are tonnes of reasons why stretches can form a valuable part of your pony's routine. It can help...
- strengthen his muscles
- improve flexibility
- increase range of motion

No matter what you do with your pony – whether it's flatwork, jumping or hacking – improving his flexibility will not only make him comfier to ride, but it'll also help him find work much easier.

Before you start

Make sure your pony's standing on a flat, firm surface, either on the yard or in his stable, and choose a time when there aren't too many distractions. You'll need to hold him with his headcollar and leadrope – or find a helper to hold him for you – and make sure he has enough room to stretch his neck either side of his body.

To encourage him to stretch, you'll also need either...
- a lick
- carrots
- treats

It's up to you which tasty treat you use, but a lick may help encourage him to hold the stretch for a bit longer. The main thing is that he really wants to reach for it!

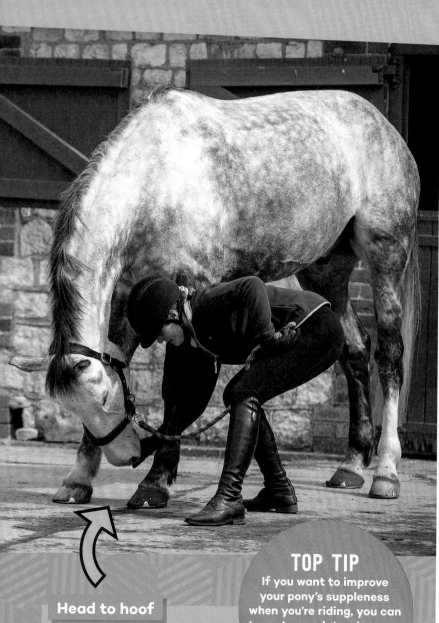

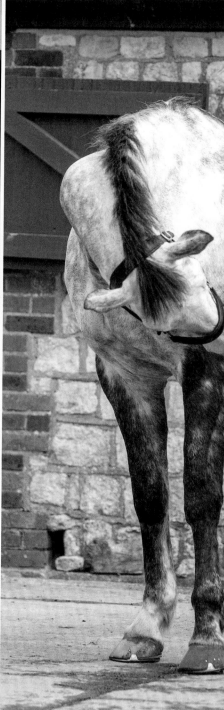

Head to hoof

The first type of stretch you can do is designed to strengthen up your horse's longitudinal suppleness – this means all the muscles across his back and top line.
These are the muscles he'll use to carry your weight while you're riding, and are the same ones that work hard when you ride him long and low.

How to do it

1. Stand beside your pony's head and make sure he's standing square.
2. Take your chosen treat and lower it down to the ground – your pony should follow it with his head.
3. Bring the treat backwards a little, so you're holding it between his forelegs. The aim is for your pony to reach his nose all the way through his forelegs to give his back and neck muscles a lovely big stretch.
4. Hold this position for around 10 seconds, then repeat a couple of times.

TOP TIP
If you want to improve your pony's suppleness when you're riding, you can try out some lateral moves, such as leg-yield and turn-on-the-forehand.

TOP TIP
For best results, try to do these stretches with your pony every day. You'll soon feel an improvement when you come to ride him!

This is the ultimate stretch to improve your pony's lateral suppleness, which is the set of muscles he uses to bend round corners and circles. You might need to build up to the full stretch gradually because it's a big ask for a pony's who's not very flexible.

How to do it
1. Stand slightly in front of your pony's flank while holding a treat.
2. Ask him to reach for the treat by flexing his neck and shoulders around his body. Only ask him to stretch as far as he's comfortable to.
3. Hold it for around 10 seconds, then repeat the stretch on his other side.

DID YOU KNOW?

If your pony needs box rest, stretches can be a great way to keep him supple while he's unable to move around.

Do the twist

You can do this next type of stretch with any pony – it encourages a little flexibility through the neck, without asking him to do too much.

How to do it
1. Stand by your pony's side with your treat of choice.
2. Encourage him to bend his neck round until his nose touches his shoulder.
3. For an extra stretch, hold the treat a bit lower down, so he stretches out the muscles on the top of his neck, too.
4. Hold it for around 10 seconds, then move round to his other side and repeat.

Stretch and flex

Working on these stretches with your pony as often as you can is sure to bring excellent results. A supple pony will find riding much more enjoyable, and building up his strength will mean you can progress more quickly, too!

PLAY THE GAME

Ready to have tonnes of fun with your pony? Give mounted games a go!

One of the most exciting things you can do with your pony has got to be mounted games! There are so many races that the possibilities are endless. Teams usually consist of four or five riders, and each member must combine skill and speed to gallop to victory and complete each race as quickly as possible. Learn all there is to know about this super-speedy sport!

DID YOU KNOW?

You can compete in mounted games as part of your local Pony Club branch, or through the Mounted Games Association.

First things first

So, how did mounted games come about? Well, it's all thanks to HRH Prince Philip! Her Majesty The Queen's late husband wanted to come up with some fun games that children with ordinary ponies could participate in at Horse of the Year Show (HOYS). So, in 1957, HOYS hosted the first mounted games championship for the Prince Philip Cup. It was a huge success, and the sport has become increasingly popular in countries around the world ever since.

Fun and games

There are dozens of different races involved in mounted games, and here are just a few examples...

- **flag fliers** Riders carry a four-foot flag, then drop it into a cone as they turn their pony. They pick up another on the way back, and pass it to the next rider
- **run and ride** Competitors race first on foot while leading their ponies, then vault up and race again while on board
- **stepping stones** Riders canter their pony towards a row of upturned buckets, jump off, hop across each one and then vault back on to ride to the finish
- **pony pairs** two riders slalom through a line of cones in tandem, while holding a rope between them
- **egg and spoon** Riders reach the finish line as fast as they can while balancing an egg on a spoon without dropping it

The right steed

Any type of pony can try mounted games, but there are a few key things to consider when selecting the perfect partner. First and foremost, they need to have a trainable attitude and be able to cope with a high level of adrenaline. They should also be speedy, brave and agile, so they can make sharp turns and quick transitions.

There's no minimum height when it comes to a mounted games pony, but the rules state that they mustn't exceed 152cm with shoes on.

DID YOU KNOW?

Some popular breeds that are favoured by top riders include Welsh ponies, Arabs, Connemaras, British Riding Ponies and Thoroughbred crosses.

TOP TIP

You can easily practise the skills required for mounted games at home! Create props with anything you have to hand, such as old buckets, cones and poles.

Smooth moves

There are some strange words you may hear to do with mounted games that all have their own meaning. These are...

- **handover** This is when one rider passes an object to the next rider of their team
- **vaulting** You'll see that mounted games riders need to be as agile as their ponies! They bounce off the ground to re-mount their ponies during a race
- **relay** This is the type of race where each rider on a team takes it in turn to race against their rivals

WIN

awesome prizes in every issue of the magazine, on Instagram, Facebook and online

Keep up to date with your fave riders and behind-the-scenes horsey action

PLUS

cute posters, fun quizzes, cringeworthy horsey fess-ups, real-life dramas and loads more!

THE COB

Is there anything the super-versatile cob can't do? From the show ring to carriage driving, they're total pros and can even turn a hoof to a very special role

We all know how special riding is. It's a chance to forget about your worries and lose yourself completely in what you're doing – it's pretty hard to stress about homework when you're enjoying a good canter!

Now imagine you have to spend a lot of time in a wheelchair or on crutches. Climbing on board is even more special, because it gives you the chance to move as fast as everyone else and gain valuable independence. At Riding for the Disabled Association (RDA) stables, incredible horses are making this magic happen every day and there's one type of pony in the spotlight.

How to spot them

You'll find all sorts of breeds at RDA centres, which source their horses and ponies from generous members of the public. But by far the most common type you'll encounter is the trusty cob.

Because cobs are a type rather than a breed, there's quite a lot of variation – while showing cobs are technically meant to be 14.2–15.1hh, you can find 13hh cobs suitable for children, and 16hh maxi-cobs, ideal for adults or heavier riders. Cobs are largely influenced by the draft breeds they were developed from, with a sturdy build, well-sized hooves, and generous necks.

Why the cob?

Cobs generally have really great temperaments, which is extra-important when they're working with people who might not be able to move so easily. They're also usually easy to take care of, because they're good-doers – and that's really helpful for the RDA, which is a charity, so it relies on support from the public.

What does it take?

First, a potential therapeutic riding horse is assessed to see if he has the right sort of temperament and is sound and safe under saddle. If he ticks all the boxes, he's then accepted for further training and evaluation, where he'll be tested for his reaction to lots of different situations. He'll learn to respond to side walkers – the volunteers who help RDA riders in lessons – and get used to sudden loud noises, mounting ramps, voice commands and much more.

The most important thing is that he's calm enough to take the unexpected in his stride. Each rider has different needs and abilities, and the horse needs to be very calm and sensible, even if his rider doesn't have much control over their own body.

DID YOU KNOW?

The RDA is run through donations and with the help of volunteers, and you don't have to be an adult to get involved. There's loads of cool stuff to do, from helping look after the ponies to assisting with lessons, and you can even work towards your Duke of Edinburgh award or a Pony Club achievement badge!

Getting competitive

RDA horses and ponies aren't plods – they're super-versatile and often have competitive backgrounds, too. That's a really helpful asset, because there are plenty of opportunities for RDA riders to compete at all levels in para-equestrian competitions, with special leagues in dressage, showjumping, driving, vaulting and much more!

TOP TIP
Choose a photo that has plenty of detail rather than lots of blank spaces. It'll make your task of putting it together more tricky, but so satisfying when it's complete!

Make
PONY PUZZLE

Turn your fave pony pic into an awesome puzzle

Sitting down with a puzzle following an epic riding lesson is a great way to relax. But the pony-themed fun doesn't have to stop when you get home from the yard. Why not have a go at following our step-by-step guide to making your own, unique pony puzzle?

You'll need

✓ card
✓ plain paper
✓ scissors
✓ glue stick
✓ pencil
✓ ruler
✓ your fave pony pic

1 Gather all the items you need and choose a high-quality photo of your pony, or the one you ride at your riding school. You could even use a poster!

2 Print out the picture on an A4 piece of paper and leave it to dry.

3 On your piece of card, measure out eight equal spaces along the short side and 12 along the long side – this will create a 96-piece puzzle!

TOP TIP
If you want to make an easier puzzle, draw bigger squares so you end up with fewer pieces.

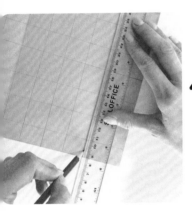

4 Draw your puzzle – the easiest way is to create a grid to make sure the pieces are even, then add in the puzzle pattern.

5 Cover the back of your printed picture in glue and stick it to the piece of card with the pattern facing outwards, so you can see it.

6 Cut out the puzzle following your guide – take care not to cut any bits off otherwise it'll be missing sections!

7 Jumble up the pieces, then you're ready for hours of puzzle fun!

Finished!

GLOBE TROTTING

Are you a whizz when it comes world breeds?
Test your knowledge with this awesome quiz

1. This quick, agile breed is often used for Western style riding, which includes herding cattle and barrel racing.

....

SOMERSET AND DEVON, UK

VIRGINIA, USA

ANDALUSIA, SPAIN

2. An Iberian beauty, these horses are mostly grey and can be seen doing classical dressage.

....

ARGENTINA, SOUTH AMERICA

3. These little fellas are known for being one of the tiniest breeds in the world.

....

4. Adorable as they are hardy, these ponies are well-known for having a dorsal stripe and creamy coloured features, known as pangaré.

....

Find these each of these breeds, then turn to p100 to find out how you got on!

■ **ANDALUSIAN**
■ **ARAB**
■ **BARB**
■ **BRUMBY**
■ **EXMOOR**
■ **FALABELLA**
■ **MARWARI**
■ **PRZEWALSKI'S HORSE**
■ **QUARTER HORSE**

I SCORED /9

5. You'll recognise this breed because of its spiky mane, and they're thought to be the last true wild horses.

....

MONGOLIA, EAST ASIA

SAUDI ARABIA

NORTH WEST INDIA

AFRICA

8. The defining feature of this breed is definitely their epic inward-curving ears!

....

6. You can't mistake this breed because of their dainty dished faces and high tail carriage.

....

QUEENSLAND, AUSTRALIA

7. Built with excellent stamina, these horses can be seen galloping across the savannah.

....

9. These horses are super-strong and roam feral down under.

....

FACING YOUR FEARS

Megan must overcome her cantering nerves so she can save the day

Every Saturday at 10.30am I go to my level three group lesson at Langston Hill Riding School. I look forward to it all week long and hope and pray that I'll get to ride my fave pony, Marble – a gorgeous strawberry roan. "Right," said my instructor Kaleigh, "today we're going to learn how to canter". *Wow!* I was super-excited – I'd always wanted to be able to canter, just like you see in films when the hero gallops to the rescue.

One by one, the others in my group had a go at cantering for the first time. All the ponies were really well-behaved, cantering along like rocking horses. Then, it was my turn. "Sit deep in the saddle, put your outside leg behind the girth and squeeze," explained Kaleigh. I did just as she said, but Marble had other ideas. Before I knew it, he'd shot off like a flash, then leapt to the side in a spook. I completely lost my balance and tumbled to the ground, smacking down right onto my bottom. I'd never fallen off before and did all I could to hold in the tears. *That's it,* I thought to myself. *I'm never cantering again.*

A downward spiral

Even though Kaleigh tried to persuade me to have another go, I point blank refused. Never again would I canter a pony. For the rest of the lesson, and the following three, I was adamant that I wouldn't ride any faster than a trot. But the rest of my group were making progress with cantering, and I was starting to fall behind. Even though I'd been given a different pony to try – a sluggish but sensible cob called Victor – I still couldn't shake off my nerves.

After a while, Mum and Dad sat me down and explained that they'd have to rethink whether to continue paying for lessons if I wasn't going to try and improve. I felt totally dejected because I still loved riding, but they just didn't understand how frustrating it felt to be crippled with nerves all the time. I wanted to carry on so badly, but the image of me thudding to the floor kept replaying in my mind. Not to mention I'd lost faith in Marble, which hurt my feelings because he'd always looked after me so well up until then.

❝ It was then that I vowed to give up riding forever ❞

Picking myself up

Just as I was starting to feel that my fears would force me to quit riding for good, something totally unexpected happened. One day after school, Mum and Dad picked me up in the car and explained that one of Dad's friends was looking for a sharer for her pony, who'd been outgrown by her daughter. Of course, I leapt at the chance. "We hope it'll help you get your confidence back," said Mum. "But it's a big commitment, so you have to promise to try your best." I nodded frantically, beaming from ear to ear.

The day I met Giuseppe was one I'll never forget. I instantly fell in love with his adorable, fluffy face and teeny-tiny ears. He was a beautiful 14hh grey – a little smaller than the ponies I'd been riding at Langston Hill, but his size made me feel like I had a bit more control when I was on his back. He was the perfect mix of calm and steady, but wasn't completely lazy either – he moved forwards off my leg from the smallest squeeze.

"Why don't you try a canter?" called Mum. I could feel the blood drain from my face. I didn't want to risk anything going wrong in case Mum and Dad changed their minds, but they were watching expectantly. Luckily, Linda, Giuseppe's owner, who was also watching, seemed to detect my nervousness and stepped in. "It's okay, we can work up to it. If you want to, of course?" she said. Immediately I grinned. *Maybe Giuseppe and Linda would be the ones to help me finally learn to canter?*

Round in circles

In the weeks that followed, Mum drove me up to the stables three days a week to ride Giuseppe. Linda gave me lessons in the school and I can't describe how much I enjoyed them. She had a way of making me feel calm and made me laugh, too, by speaking in a funny voice as if it was Giuseppe talking.

She suggested that I have some lunge lessons to help get my confidence up. I'd never had one before, but doing

funny things like swinging my arms around like a windmill, reaching down to touch my toes and even riding without stirrups was the most fun I'd ever had on a pony. It was even better because Linda had full control of Giuseppe on the end of the lunge line, so I felt a bit safer.

After a few sessions, when my trust in Giuseppe had grown, Linda decided I was ready to try a canter on the lunge. Swallowing my nerves, I agreed to give it a go. Linda clicked Giuseppe on, and I felt myself tense up. My anxious brain made me clench the reins really tightly and my upper body curled forwards. But this only made Giuseppe confused, so he did a little buck, which felt enormous. Because my position had gone so awry, I plopped straight over his head and, once again, ended up on the floor. I felt even worse when a young boy walked his pony past the arena and said to his mum, "I can't believe she can't canter at her age," probably not intending for me to hear. It was then that I vowed to give up riding forever.

On the run

No matter how much I insisted that I wanted to stop sharing Giuseppe, my parents kept saying I had to give it one more try. In my heart, I knew it had been my fault that I'd fallen off – Giuseppe just picked up on my nerves. I owed it to him to keep going.

Next time I went to the stables I was very quiet and unsure, so Linda suggested we go for an amble round some of the local bridlepaths. That way, I could enjoy spending time in the saddle without the pressures of the arena. I'd only been on a few hacks at the riding school so felt a little apprehensive, but hacking was the best thing ever! Linda and I had a great chat while she walked beside me and Giuseppe, and I loved being out in the open exploring the countryside. We even managed a little trot down a woodland track.

Just as we stepped out onto the edge of an open field, Giuseppe pricked his ears. There was something moving in the distance. "Help!" came a cry from the far side. It was a pony and rider trotting completely out of control. "That's Kevin!" exclaimed Linda – he was the young boy from the stables. Kevin's exhausted mum was running after him – the pony had obviously broken free from the leadrein. "Help me!" he cried.

All of a sudden, something switched within me. I knew I was the only one who could catch up to him. "I'll go," I said, squeezing Giuseppe into a trot across the field. Even though we were trotting fast, we weren't gaining enough ground. Kevin's pony had

broken into canter, and they were heading towards the open gate.

Not having a chance to think, I grabbed a handful of mane, nudged Giuseppe into canter and charged after them. Giuseppe surged across the open grass and the wind roared in my ears – I'd never been so fast. Amazingly, I was so focused on Kevin that I didn't feel at all scared.

Giuseppe was quick and we managed to catch up with Kevin and his pony, Marigold. "You've got to pull the reins!" I yelled to him, but Kevin was so panicked that he wasn't listening at all. "Pull!" I yelled again, and this time he managed to lean back and tug the reins until Marigold came back to trot, and then walk. I jumped off and grabbed his reins, leading both ponies back to the adults. Kevin was sobbing by the time we got to his mum, who gave him a big hug. Linda gave me a pat on the back, smiling proudly. Not only had I saved Kevin, I'd also had my very first canter, and now I couldn't wait to do it again.

Up, up and away

After my accidental canter, I couldn't get enough. I wanted to canter everywhere and Giuseppe was loving going on adventures with the other liveries at the yard. I took him for long rides in the woods, across fields with excellent canter tracks and one day we even loaded up into the horsebox for a beach ride, which was incredible. My nerves are a thing of the past now, and I have my sights set on learning to jump next.

YOUR ANNUAL *quiz*

How much have you learnt from your annual?
Take our quiz to find out

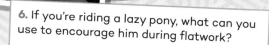

1. Who's the youngest jockey evet to win the Shetland Pony Grand National?

....

2. How many police horses are in the mounted section?

....

3. Which breed is the most popular choice for scurry racing?

....

4. What's a good exercise to try if you're riding a strong pony?

....

5. How much weight might a drum horse carry in a ceremony?

....

6. If you're riding a lazy pony, what can you use to encourage him during flatwork?

....

7. What are three ways you can check your pony's weight?

....

8. In which showing class do you ride over fences?

....

9. What's the tallest a pony is allowed to be to compete in mounted games?

....

10. What should you avoid using on your pony's mane before you plait?

....

I SCORED

/10

HOW DID YOU GET ON?
To check your answers, scan the code or visit
bit.ly/PNY_QUIZ_ANSWERS

GLOBE TROTTING ANSWERS P96

1. Quarter horse – Virginia, North America **2. Andalusian** – Spain **3. Falabella** – Argentina, South America
4. Exmoor – Exmoor, UK **5. Przwalski's horse** – Mongolia, East Asia **6. Arab** – Saudi Arabia **7. Barb** – Africa
8. Marwari – North West India **9. Brumby** – Queensland, Australia

PONY PORTRAIT CAKE

P20

Template

This template is at full size and will fit a 20cm cake tin.

Trace this pony portrait onto greaseproof paper. If you prefer, you can download it at **bit.ly/ANNUAL_BAKE_TEMPLATE** or scan the code!

DID YOU KNOW?

The finished cake will come out as a mirror image of the template you traced!

THE MISADVENTURES OF CHARLIE!